Teacher's Book
STARTER

Christina de la Mare

Contents

Introduction

Teaching notes

Workbook answer key

Introduction

Introducing *Champions*

Methodology

Champions is a new four-level British English course written specifically for secondary school students, with particular emphasis on meaningful communication and skills development.

These are the key features of *Champions* methodology.

Hands-on language presentation Students immediately interact with the dialogue or text that opens each unit, checking their understanding of meaning and context, and giving them the chance to try out new structures.

Guided discovery Students explore the meaning and usage of new language before they move on to more formal presentation and practice.

Communicative practice Dialogue work and personalization are emphasized at each level, and pairwork activities and games are included throughout.

Cultural awareness A focus on the UK and other English-speaking countries is placed within the context of the wider world.

Skills development In every unit students apply and extend what they have learned, through targeted skills lessons designed to build their competence in each individual skill.

Self-assessment Students regularly review and measure their progress against the Common European Framework of Reference.

Learning across the curriculum Inter-disciplinary reading and project pages link the topics and language content of the main units to other areas of the school curriculum.

Values The topics in *Champions* have been carefully chosen to stimulate reflection on a broad range of issues related to citizenship and the development of socially responsible values. These are highlighted in the teaching notes for each unit.

Flexibility

A comprehensive and innovative package of components gives the teacher maximum support and flexibility. Whatever your teaching style, *Champions* has everything you could possibly need to match your students' learning environment.

Combined Student's Book and Workbook available as a combined edition

Student CD-ROM with many hours of interactive material for home practice, including extra listening activities

Flexible assessment options Printable, editable tests are included on the Teacher's Resource disc, including a **KET practice test** for level 3 of *Champions*. Further practice tests can be purchased from oxfordenglishtesting.com

Printable worksheets 38 extra worksheets are included on each Teacher's Resource disc, including pairwork activities and games, and review and extension worksheets for extra grammar and vocabulary practice

Overview of components

Student's Book and Workbook

The Student's Book contains:
- six teaching units
- a Welcome unit, reviewing key language from the previous level. In the Starter level, the Welcome unit briefly reviews basic language typically covered at primary level
- vocabulary and grammar review after every two units, including 'can do' statements correlated to the Common European Framework of Reference to encourage regular self-assessment
- a Culture club lesson in each Review unit, giving an insight into life in the UK and other English-speaking countries
- three Curriculum extra reading and project lessons.

The Workbook contains:
- additional practice for each unit, covering grammar, vocabulary, communication, reading, and writing
- detailed grammar notes included at the start of each Workbook unit for ease of reference.

Student's CD-ROM

The Student's CD-ROM contains:
- extra interactive practice for each vocabulary, grammar and communication lesson from the Student's Book
- extra listening practice
- interactive games.

Teacher's Book

The Teacher's Book contains:
- teaching notes and answer keys for all the Student's Book material
- ideas for warm-ups and extra activities
- suggestions for using authentic songs with specific topics or areas of language
- background notes and cultural information on people and topics mentioned in the Student's Book
- audio scripts for all listening material
- answer keys for all the Workbook material.

Class Audio CDs

Each set of Class Audio CDs contains:
- all the listening material for the Student's Book.

Teacher's Resource Disc

The Teacher's Resource Disc contains:
- six unit tests and three review tests
- thirty-six photocopiables worksheets, including pairwork activities and games, and review and extension worksheets for extra grammar and vocabulary practice
- audio for review tests. and vocabulary extension worksheets

Using the Student's Book

Welcome unit

The Welcome unit offers six pages of vocabulary and grammar practice, covering language students have seen in the previous level. In the Starter level, students are given a brief overview of basic language they may have seen at primary level, before beginning the main syllabus in Unit 1.

Main units

Each main unit is divided as follows:

Presentation 2 pages

Vocabulary 1 page

Grammar 1 page

Communication 1 page

Grammar 1 page

Skills 2 pages

Presentation

The presentation text on the left-hand page exposes students to the theme, grammar, vocabulary, and functions of the unit. The exercises on the right-hand page allow students to interact with the dialogue in more detail, encouraging them to explore, use, and personalize new language before it is formally presented and practised on the Vocabulary and Grammar pages.

In the Starter level and Level 1, the text is a dialogue presented in a photostory format. The photostories reflect the aspirations of the students, using familiar contexts to motivate and engage them. Each unit focuses on a different episode in the lives of the central characters.

In the Starter level, the story takes place in a performing arts school and follows the fortunes of a new student, Holly. Holly is happy to be at her new school and quickly makes friends, but she also finds that she has a rival who wants to prevent her from achieving her dreams. The story culminates in the production of a school musical, where Holly finally wins the lead role.

In Level 1, we follow the story of Sam. Sam loves basketball, but he is having problems with poor grades in his other school subjects. As he faces a moral dilemma, he is helped by a friend to make the right choice, and in the end everything works out for the best.

In Levels 2 and 3, the emphasis is on texts dealing with individual topics of a more grown-up nature, in recognition of the fact that students, along with their interests and tastes, mature very quickly during the teenage years. A variety of formats and genres is used, including dialogues, magazine articles, and web pages.

Following on from the presentation text, students complete a series of questions to check basic comprehension. The **Check it out!** feature draws students' attention to useful colloquial expressions in the dialogue.

Language focus

The exercises in the Language focus section familiarize students with the language of the unit, without requiring them to manipulate it. In Starter and Level 1, students focus on the target language in relation to specific scenes and sections of dialogue from the photostory; in Levels 2 and 3, students find phrases and structures in the presentation text and use them to complete sentences or captions about the text.

Finally, **Focus on you** and **Pairwork** activities give students the chance to try out the new language in a personalized context, following carefully controlled models.

Vocabulary

This page presents and practices a set of vocabulary items associated with the unit topic and previewed in the presentation lesson. **Look!** boxes contain useful tips and draw attention to potential pitfalls, including spelling rules, exceptions or irregular forms, collocations, and notes about English usage.

Students once again have the opportunity for guided speaking practice with a **Pairwork** activity at the end of the lesson.

At the foot of the Vocabulary page students are directed to the Student's CD-ROM and the Workbook, where there is further practice of the unit vocabulary.

Grammar

Underlying the methodology of *Champions* is the conviction that students understand and remember rules better if they work them out for themselves. As a result, a guided discovery approach to teaching grammar is adopted throughout the series.

Each unit has two Grammar lessons. A grammar chart models the form of the key structures, using examples taken from the presentation text that opens the unit.

Having already experimented with the new structures earlier in the unit, students are encouraged to reflect on correct usage in more detail as they complete the **Think!** activity.

A cross-reference to **Rules** then directs the students to a grammar reference page in the corresponding Workbook unit, where detailed explanations and examples are given.

The activities on the page provide thorough and detailed practice of both form and usage, moving from carefully controlled exercises to more demanding production.

Each Grammar page has an optional **Finished?** activity. These are designed as a fun way of providing extension work for fast finishers.

One Grammar page in each unit also features a **Game** that encourages personalized practice in a less formal context.

At the end of each Grammar page students are directed to the Student's CD-ROM and the Workbook, where there is further practice.

Communication

One page in every unit focuses on everyday English. Conversational language is presented in the form of a dialogue which reviews the vocabulary and grammar from the previous lessons. In a similar way to the Language focus lesson on page 2 of the unit, Communication lessons allow students to explore and use a new structure before they move on to more formal practice on the subsequent Grammar page.

The **You ask/You answer** feature summarizes the target language in the dialogue, while a **Pronunciation** activity draws students' attention to a specific sound or a relevant aspect of intonation. The students then listen to this language in different contexts before practising it themselves in the **Pairwork** activity.

At the end of each Communication page students are directed to the Student's CD-ROM and the Workbook, where there is further practice.

Skills

The last two pages of the unit contain targeted skills work designed to equip students with the necessary strategies to build confidence and competence in each individual skill.

Skills lessons also provide a way of consolidating and recycling the language students have studied throughout the unit, whilst exploring different aspects of the unit topic.

Reading texts deal with the main topic of the unit in a factual way using real-life contexts. Comprehension exercises typical start with a skimming or scanning activity, followed by more detailed questions that gradually increase in difficulty as the series progresses.

Listening activities extend the topic of the text. A variety of activity formats is used to help students develop well-rounded listening comprehension skills.

The Speaking and Writing sections give students the opportunity to respond to the unit topic with their own ideas. To help students to organize their ideas, both sections usually begin with a written preparation stage. The aim is to strike a balance between giving clear, guided models on the page on the one hand, and allowing students freedom to express themselves and experiment with newly-acquired vocabulary and structures on the other.

Review units

After every two main units there is a two-page Review unit comprising:

Grammar and Vocabulary review and **My Progress** +1 page

Culture club reading 1 page

The first half of each Review unit covers the main grammar and vocabulary points from the previous two units. The **My Progress** chart is a self-assessment chart correlated to the Common European Framework of Reference. It is very motivating for students to reflect on their progress and this type of activity is also very helpful in encouraging students to take responsibility for their own learning.

Most teenagers are curious to know what life is like for their peers in other parts of the world. **Culture club** reading lessons give a factual account of different aspects of the English-speaking world from a young person's perspective. The **Focus on you** section at the end of the lesson invites a personal response from students in the form of a piece of writing.

Curriculum extra

There are four cross-curricular reading and project lessons in the Student's Book, providing two pages of material for each block of four units. The Curriculum extra lessons link to the themes of the corresponding Student's Book units, as well as to subjects that students typically study in their own language, such as geography, science, maths, art, and history.

Each of the lessons concludes with a project that synthesizes the language focus and the content of the cross-curricular theme and gives students the opportunity to develop their creativity. The projects can be done in class or assigned for homework. Depending on time available and the needs of the students, the projects can be done in groups, pairs, or individually.

Workbook

The Workbook section contains six five-page units of extra practice of the language and skills taught in the Student's Book. The Workbook exercises can be completed in class or for homework.

The first two pages of each Workbook unit summarize the grammar structures introduced in the corresponding Student's Book unit with comprehensive charts and detailed grammar notes.

The following two pages provide extra vocabulary and grammar practice. The last two pages provide additional practice to accompany the Student's Book Communication lesson, and further reading and writing practice.

Student's CD-ROM

The Student's CD-ROM contains interactive practice of the Grammar, Vocabulary and Communication sections of each unit of the Student's Book.

For each Student's Book unit there are eight grammar activities and two vocabulary exercises, and a communication exercise with audio. Communication exercises feature extra audio based on the corresponding Student's Book dialogues.

From each screen students can click to access a **wordlist** with audio to listen to the vocabulary from the corresponding Student's Book unit.

There are two games for every two units. The first, in which students have to identify the odd one out, practises vocabulary; in the second game students play against an opponent and have to complete correct grammatical sentences. For each game, there are three levels of difficulty.

Teacher's Book

The Teacher's Book contains detailed lesson notes and answers for all the Student's Book and Workbook material.

Each Teacher's Book unit starts with a summary of the areas of vocabulary, grammar, communication, skills, and topical themes covered in the Student Book unit. Also listed are themes relating to values and responsible citizenship, such as:

- Ethics and morals
- Society, including the themes of respect, solidarity, and justice
- Multiculturalism, including anthropology, human rights, cultural studies, sociology, and historical, geographical, legal, and ethical perspectives
- The environment, including protecting the environment, and natural cycles
- Work and consumerism, including mass communication, advertising, sales, workers' rights, and consumer rights
- Health.

The notes include a description of the aim of every exercise in the Student's Book, followed by detailed instructions and answers.

There are also suggestions for Warm-up activities, and Extra activities that can be used to extend the Student's Book content according to the needs and abilities of each class.

The Student's Book is full of factual information and references to the real world. The teaching notes provide support for this by giving additional notes and cultural facts in the **Background information**.

Teenage students have an insatiable interest in music and popular culture, and the use of songs to consolidate the linguistic and topical content of the Student's Book can be an effective way of motivating students.

The teaching notes for each Review unit include suggestions for suitable songs that can be exploited for this purpose. The songs have been chosen because of their lexical, grammatical, or thematic link to the corresponding units.

See page 8 for suggestions on how to exploit songs in class.

Class Audio CD

The Class Audio CD is for classroom use. There is a track list on page 13.

Extra resources

Alongside the Student's Book and Workbook, there is a large amount of extra resource material included on Teacher's Resource Disc. The extra resources provide support material for consolidation, extension, mixed ability classes, and assessment. All resources are printable, and can also be projected in class.

Tests

For each level of *Champions*, there are six unit tests and three review tests, all of which can be opened using Microsoft® Word and edited before printing.

The unit tests include vocabulary and grammar questions, dialogue work, and a writing task. Each test is scored out of 50 points.

The review tests focus on vocabulary and grammar, and reading, writing and listening skills. Each test is scored out of 100 points.

Regular assessment makes it easier to monitor students' progress. Teachers can keep a record of individual students' progress using the evaluation chart on page 12.

Grammar and vocabulary

Grammar help and **Vocabulary help** worksheets for each unit provide additional practice of the Student's Book material at a basic level, and are ideal for giving weaker students more practice.

Grammar extension and **Vocabulary extension** worksheets offer more challenging practice for the more able students.

Pairwork

There is one pairwork worksheet per unit, giving oral practice of the grammar and vocabulary of the corresponding unit.

Puzzles and games

One page of puzzles is included for each unit, and two board games for each level of the series. Although these resources give practice of the main grammar and vocabulary of the unit, the emphasis is on fun activities, such as crosswords, wordsearches, and code breakers.

Practice test for Cambridge ESOL examinations

Level 3 of *Champions* Teacher's Resource Disc includes a KET practice test.

Classroom management

An English-speaking environment

- Use English for classroom instructions as often as you can, and ask students to use English as well. For example: *Open your books at page 10. Let's look at exercise 3. Raise your hand. Work in pairs. Ask your partner*, etc.
- Students should be encouraged to use expressions such as: *How do you say … in English? How do you spell …? I don't understand. Please can you repeat that? Can you say that more slowly, please? Can we listen to that again, please? Can I go to the toilet?*

Managing large classes

Large classes are easier to manage if you establish routines such as:

- Write a plan of the day's activities on the board.
- Make sure that everyone understands the task before they start. Give clear examples and ask students to provide a few as well.
- Set time limits for all activities and remind students of time limits, for example: *You have two minutes left.*
- Walk around the class, monitoring while students work.
- Get to know your students' personalities and learning styles so that you can maximize their potential in class.
- Allow stronger students to help weaker students while ensuring that there is always an atmosphere of mutual respect and understanding.

Group and pairwork

The interaction from working in small groups or in pairs is vital in a language classroom, and students quickly get used to what to expect. Here are some tips for organizing group work in large classes:

- Don't have more than five students per group.
- Set up group activities quickly by allocating students with a letter (A, B, C, etc.). Students form groups with other students who have the same letter.
- Demonstrate tasks with one pair or group at the front of the class.
- Set a time limit and keep reminding students of it.

Songs

There are many ways in which songs can be exploited in class, including the following suggestions:

- **Gap-fill** There are many variations of this type of activity, in which students are given the lyrics with certain key words deleted. To make it easier for students, the missing words can be grouped together in a wordpool. As students read the lyrics, they try to fill in the gaps, then they listen and check. If you wish to make the activity more challenging, you could add extra words to the wordpool as distracters, or not provide the missing words at all. It is important to choose the gapped words carefully, however, both so that they are audible, and so that students can guess from the context which word makes most sense in each gap.

- **Correct the mistakes** Include some incorrect words or information in the lyrics. Ask students to identify where the mistakes are and replace them with the correct words, before they listen to the song to check their answers.
- **Choose the correct alternative** At regular points in the lyrics, students have to choose between two or more alternative words or phrases to complete the lyrics correctly. Students then listen and check.
- **Put the verses in the correct order** This activity works especially well with songs that tell a story. Students are given the verses in the wrong order, and they have to guess the correct order before listening to the song.
- **Match rhyming words** Many songs are structured so that alternating lines end with rhyming words, and this provides an excellent opportunity to work on different sounds. One useful activity is to give students the lyrics with the lines of each verse jumbled. Students then attempt to unjumble the lines, according to which lines rhyme with each other, before listening to the song to check their ideas. Another variation is for students to choose between two alternatives to end each line. This could mean choosing the word that provides the best rhyme, for example, or the word that makes most sense in the context.
- **Match words to definitions:** Songs often contain informal expressions, idioms, and 'untidy' grammar. With stronger groups it can be useful to have students try to match difficult words and expressions to definitions or explanations. Alternatively, where lyrics feature more standard items of vocabulary, students could work together in groups to find the words in a dictionary and agree on a definition.

Feedback

It is important for students to have a sense of how they have performed. Provide feedback while you are monitoring activities. Alternatively, you can assess an exercise afterwards with the whole class: students can put up their hands to indicate how many answers they shared in pairs or groups, how hard or easy the task was, etc.

Encourage students to behave well using a points system. Award points to pairs or groups that don't make too much noise. Deduct points from pairs or groups that are too noisy or who are not speaking in English.

Suggestions for further reading

General reference

Oxford Essential Learner's Dictionary – New Edition
Practice English Usage – 3rd Edition by Michael Swan

Grammar

The Good Grammar Book (Elementary to Lower-Intermediate) by Michael Swan and Catherine Walter

Graded readers

The Oxford Bookworms Library (Elementary to Pre-intermediate) – non-fiction readers that are ideal for extended reading, and graded non-fiction readers that are ideal for cultural and cross-curricular studies.

Exam preparation

KET PRACTICE TESTS – New Edition

Ideas for supplementary activities and teacher development

Oxford Basics – a series of short, accessible books for teachers who are looking for new creative ways of teaching with limited resources.

Resource Books for Teachers – a popular series that give teachers practical advice and guidance, together with resource ideas and materials for the classroom.

Games to use in the classroom

Kim's Game

On a tray, place a selection of objects from a vocabulary set, e.g. classroom objects or food. Alternatively, you can write the names of the objects on the board and rub them off.

In groups, give students two minutes to memorize what is on the tray or board.

Remove an object and ask students to write down the missing object. Continue until the tray or board is empty.

Check the answers with the class. The group with all the objects in the correct order is the winner.

Simon Says

Call out commands to the class. If your command is preceded by 'Simon says', students must obey the instruction. If it is not, they must ignore it. For example: *Simon says stand up.* (students stand up) *Sit down.* (students remain standing). Students who get it wrong are out of the game. This activity is good primarily for practising imperatives, but is also useful for practising vocabulary. With a strong class, you could let a student call out the commands.

Bingo

Tell each student to draw a grid of six squares and refer them to the vocabulary page(s) you have just worked on. Give them a few moments to memorize the words and pictures in the vocabulary set.

Books closed, students then draw or write a vocabulary item in each square. Call out vocabulary items from the set. If the students have drawn pictures, call out the words in English. If students have written the English words, you can call them out in their L1. With a strong class you could read out definitions and get students to work out the word.

When a student hears a word he or she has drawn or written, they must cross it out. When all six vocabulary items are crossed out, the student can call out *Bingo*. The first to call out *Bingo* wins the game.

Hangman

Choose a word or phrase. Write a gap for each letter of the word on the board. Separate words with a clear space or slash, e.g. *I lived in Paris.* _ / _ _ _ _ _ / _ _ / _ _ _ _ _
Students guess which letters appear in the words. Each student can call out just one letter. If the letter is contained in the word, or phrase, write it in the appropriate place(s), e.g. for the letter 'i': I / _ i _ _ _ / i _ / _ _ _ i _ .

If a student calls out a letter that isn't in the word or phrase, write it on the board and draw one line of the hangman.

If students guess the word or phrase before the hangman is drawn completely, they have won. If they do not, you are the winner. This can be played on the board with the whole class, in small groups, or in pairs.

The complete drawing should look like this.

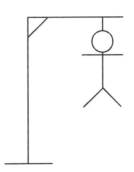

20 Questions

This can be played on the board with the whole class, in small groups, or in pairs. One student chooses a secret identity, e.g. that of a celebrity. Other students must guess the identity by asking a maximum of 20 questions. The student may only answer with short yes / no answers, e.g. *Yes, I am. No, I don't*, etc. The game can be used to practise questions and answers in a variety of different tenses.

Chinese Whispers

This game is excellent for practising pronunciation. It can be played as a whole class or in small groups of at least six. Put students in a line or circle. Write a sentence on a piece of paper and give it to the first student. They should read it silently, but not show it to anyone else. The student then whispers the sentence to the person on their left, and so on. The game continues until the last student whispers the sentence in the first student's ear. The first student then tells the whole group / class what he or she heard, and then reads out the original sentence. Is it the same?

Common European Framework of Reference (CEFR)

The Common European Framework of Reference (CEFR) was designed to promote a consistent interpretation of foreign-language competence among the member states of the European Union. Today, the use of the CEFR has expanded beyond the boundaries of Europe, and it is used in other regions of the world, including Latin America, Asia, and the Middle East.

The CEFR defines linguistic competence in three levels: A, B, and C. Each of these levels is split into two sub-levels:

A	Basic User	A1	Breakthrough
		A2	Waystage
B	Independent User	B1	Threshold
		B2	Vantage
C	Proficient User	C1	Effectiveness
		C2	Mastery

The CEFR provides teachers with a structure for assessing their students' progress as well as monitoring specific language objectives and achievements. Students respond to the CEFR statements in the Reviews after Units 2, 4, 6, and 8.

Champions aims to enable students to move from no English or level A1 and into level B2 at the end of the four years of the course.

Descriptions of the CEFR levels covered in *Champions*

Basic User

A1 Can understand and use familiar everyday expressions and very basic phrases aimed at the satisfaction and needs of a concrete type. Can introduce him/herself and others and can ask and answer questions about personal details such as where he/she lives, people he/she knows, and things he/she has. Can interact in a simple way provided the other person talks slowly and clearly and is prepared to help.

A2 Can understand sentences and frequently used expressions related to areas of most immediate relevance (e.g. very basic personal and family information, shopping, geography, employment). Can communicate in simple and routine tasks requiring a simple and direct exchange of information on familiar and routine matters. Can describe in simple terms aspect of his/her background, immediate environment, and matters in areas of immediate need.

Independent User

B1 Can understand the main points of clear standard input on familiar matters regularly encountered in work, school, leisure, etc. Can deal with most situations likely to arise whilst travelling in an area where the language is spoken. Can produce simple connected text on topics which are familiar or of personal interest. Can describe experiences and events, dreams, hopes and ambitions, and briefly give reasons and explanations for opinions and plans.

B2 Can understand the main ideas of complex text on both concrete and abstract topics, including technical discussions in his/her field of specialization. Can interact with a degree of fluency and spontaneity that makes regular interaction with native speakers quite possible without strain for either party. Can produce clear, detailed text on a wide range of subjects and explain a viewpoint on a topical issue giving the advantages and disadvantages of various options.

Language Portfolio

The Language Portfolio has been developed in conjunction with the CEFR. It is kept by each student and contains details their language learning experiences.

There are three elements to a Language Portfolio:

A Language Biography

This can consist of the following

- Checklists for students to assess their own language skills in terms of 'What I can do'. In the Student's Book, these are found in the Review Units after Units 2, 4 and 6. Alternatively there are Portfolio pages in the Teacher's Book on pages 58-87
- A Student's self-assessment checklist to help student evaluate what they remember. See the photocopiable form for students on page 11
- A worksheet to help students identify their objectives. See the photocopiable form for students on page 11
- A checklist for students of learning activities they can do outside the classroom. See the photocopiable form for students on page 11

A Language Passport

This is an overview of the level attained by the student in English at the end of the year, for example an end-of-year report from the teacher.

A Dossier

This consists of samples of the student's work, including tests, written work, projects, or other student-generated materials.

Student's self-assessment checklist

What I remember

Useful grammar:

_____

_____

_____

_____

_____

Useful vocabulary:

_____

_____

_____

_____

_____

Objectives

One thing I need to improve:

_____

_____

_____

_____

How can I improve this?

_____

_____

_____

_____

What did you do in English outside class?

_____ Do homework

_____ Learn new words

_____ Revise before a test

_____ Listen to music

_____ Read something extra in English

_____ Watch a TV programme, video, or DVD

_____ Write an email or chat

_____ Look at web pages

_____ Speak to someone in English

_____ Read a magazine

Other activities

_____

_____

_____

_____

_____

_____

Student's progress record sheet

Name _____

Class / Year _____

Class work: continuous assessment					Test results
	Date	Grammar	Vocabulary	Skills	
Unit 1					
Unit 2					
Unit 3					
Unit 4					
Unit 5					
Unit 6					

	Comments
Units 1–2	
Units 3–4	
Units 5–6	

Class Audio CD track list

Contents

Track	Contents
01	Title

Welcome unit

02	Page 4, Exercise 1
03	Page 4, Exercise 2
04	Page 4, Exercise 3
05	Page 4, Exercise 5
06	Page 5, Exercise 1
07	Page 5, Exercise 4
08	Page 6, Exercise 1
09	Page 6, Exercise 3
10	Page 7, Exercise 2
11	Page 7, Exercise 3
12	Page 7, Exercise 4
13	Page 10, Exercise 1
14	Page 10, Exercise 2

Unit 1 Is she your friend?

15	Page 12, Exercise 1
16	Page 13, Exercise 4
17	Page 14, Exercise 1
18	Page 16, Exercise 1
19	Page 16, Exercise 2
20	Page 19, Exercise 2

Unit 2 Have you got a mobile phone?

21	Page 20, Exercise 1
22	Page 21, Exercise 4
23	Page 22, Exercise 1
24	Page 24, Exercise 1
25	Page 24, Exercise 2
26	Page 24, Exercise 3
27	Page 27, Exercise 2

Unit 3 We get up at seven

28	Page 30, Exercise 1
29	Page 31, Exercise 4
30	Page 32, Exercise 1
31	Page 33, Exercise 3
32	Page 33, Exercise 4
33	Page 34, Exercise 1
34	Page 34, Exercise 2
35	Page 37, Exercise 2

Unit 4 Do you like your new school?

36	Page 38, Exercise 1
37	Page 39, Exercise 4
38	Page 40, Exercise 1
39	Page 42, Exercise 1
40	Page 42, Exercise 2
41	Page 45, Exercise 3

Unit 5 I can sing very well

42	Page 48, Exercise 1
43	Page 49, Exercise 4
44	Page 50, Exercise 1
45	Page 51, Exercise 3
46	Page 51, Exercise 4
47	Page 52, Exercise 1
48	Page 52, Exercise 2
49	Page 55, Exercise 2

Unit 6 What's she doing now?

50	Page 56, Exercise 1
51	Page 57, Exercise 4
52	Page 58, Exercise 1
53	Page 60, Exercise 1
54	Page 60, Exercise 2
55	Page 60, Exercise 3
56	Page 63, Exercise 2

Contents

Asking and answering personal questions **Pronunciation:** Falling intonation in *Wh-* questions	**Reading:** The Star Academy staff **Listening:** An interview with a teacher **Speaking:** Role play an interview **Writing:** A personal profile
Talking about possessions **Pronunciation:** /h/	**Reading:** The perfect celebrity family **Listening:** Jack's family **Speaking:** Describe *The Simpsons* family **Writing:** Celebrity family

Curriculum extra: Social science page 66

Talking about TV programmes **Pronunciation:** Falling intonation in *Wh-* questions	**Reading:** A Musical Sensation **Listening:** Daily routine **Speaking:** Describe your daily routine **Writing:** Your favourite day of the week

Talking about likes and dislikes
Pronunciation: Rising intonation in
   yes/no questions and falling intonation
   in *Wh-* questions
	Reading: Hannah swims to success
	Listening: Mark talking about his school
	Speaking: Ask and answer questions about sports
	Writing: Your favourite school day and sports

Curriculum extra: Biology page 67

Making suggestions **Pronunciation:** Intonation in phrases	**Reading:** Superheroes **Listening:** A radio interview **Speaking:** Ask and answer questions about things you can do **Writing:** Free time and abilities
Money and shopping for clothes **Pronunciation:** /i:/ /i/	**Reading:** Let's Go! Summer Camp **Listening:** A telephone conversation **Speaking:** Describe what people are doing **Writing:** A postcard from your holiday

Curriculum extra: History page 68

Welcome

Grammar

Question words

Subject pronouns

be: present simple

Possessive adjectives

Singulars and plurals (*a / an*)

there is / there are

Vocabulary

The alphabet, Numbers, Colours, Classroom objects, Time, Days and months, Seasons, Introductions, Countries and nationalities

The alphabet   page 4

Aims

To review the pronunciation of the alphabet; to ask what someone's name is, and to say and spell their own name

Warm-up

• Hold up some classroom objects for students to spell the words.

Exercise 1  02

• Play the CD. Students listen and repeat each letter chorally, then individually.

Transcript   Student's Book page 4

Exercise 2  03

• Play the CD. Students listen and write the name of the people under the photos.

• Check the answers with the class.

ANSWERS / AUDIO CD TRACK 03

1 Amy. A-M-Y.

2 Joel. J-O-E-L.

3 Rebecca. R-E-B-E-C-C-A.

4 Ryan. R-Y-A-N.

Exercise 3  04

• Play the CD. Students listen and read.

• Students listen again and repeat chorally, then individually.

Transcript   Student's Book page 4

Exercise 4 Pairwork

• In pairs, students practise asking and answering about their name with a partner. Refer them back to exercise 3.

ANSWERS

Students' own answers.

Extra activity

• Team game. Divide the class into two teams, A and B. Call out the names of famous film and pop stars for students to spell their names.

• Teams get one point for each correct answer. The team with the most points wins.

Numbers   page 4

Aims

To review numbers from 1 to 30; to say how old students are

Exercise 5 05

• Students match the words in the box with the missing numbers.

• Play the CD. Students listen and check.

• Students listen again and repeat each number chorally, then individually.

ANSWERS / AUDIO CD TRACK 05

6 six   9 nine   14 fourteen   18 eighteen

21 twenty-one   25 twenty-five

Transcript   Student's Book page 4

Extra activity

• Play *Bingo* as a class. Students write down four numbers between 1 and 30.

• Call out numbers between 1 and 30, making a note of the ones you call out.

• The first student who matches all the numbers you have called out is the winner.

• You can repeat the game a few times.

Exercise 6

• Make sure students understand *plus* (+), *minus* (-), *times* (x), and *divided by* (÷).

• Students complete the sums.

• Check the answers with the class.

ANSWERS

2 twenty   3 twelve   4 thirty   5 eleven   6 fourteen

7 eight   8 twenty-three

Exercise 7 Pairwork

• Ask a student *How old are you?* and elicit the correct answer.

• In pairs, students ask and answer about their age. Monitor for correct use of the verb *be* in the question and answer and review as necessary.

ANSWERS

Students' own answers.

Colours page 5

Aims
To review the words for colours; to understand colour combinations; to ask and answer about their favourite colours

Warm-up
- Hold up some classroom objects and ask students what colour they are.

Exercise 1 06
- Students match the words in the box with the colours.
- Play the CD. Students listen and check.
- Students listen again and repeat chorally, then individually.

ANSWERS / AUDIO CD TRACK 06

purple   **1** brown   **2** blue   **3** pink   **4** red   **5** orange
6 black   **7** green   **8** white   **9** yellow

Exercise 2
- Go through the example as a class, making sure that students understand how to work out the colour sums.
- Students work out the other sums.
- Check the answers with the class.

ANSWERS

1 green   **2** blue   **3** orange   **4** red   **5** brown
6 yellow

Exercise 3 Pairwork
- In pairs, students ask and answer about their favourite colours.
- Ask for class feedback. Is there a favourite colour in the class?

> **Extra activity**
> - In pairs, S1 has the book open and S2 has it closed. S1 looks at the colours in exercise 2 and says, e.g. *green*. S2 should then say *blue plus yellow*. Or S1 says the colour combination and S2 says the colour.

Classroom objects page 5

Aim
To review some common classroom objects

Warm-up
- Hold up one or two classroom objects and see if students remember their names.

Exercise 4 07
- Students match the words in the box with the pictures.
- Play the CD. Students listen and check.
- Students listen again and repeat chorally, then individually.

ANSWERS / AUDIO CD TRACK 07

crayon   **1** felt tip   **2** ruler   **3** rubber   **4** pencil case
5 pencil   **6** pen   **7** rucksack   **8** exercise book
9 pencil sharpener

Exercise 5
- Students complete the words with the missing letters.
- Check the answers with the class.

ANSWERS

1 felt tip   **2** ruler   **3** exercise book   **4** pencil case
5 rucksack

Exercise 6 Pairwork
- In pairs, students talk about the objects in exercise 4.
- Monitor and check that students are taking turns to describe the classroom objects, and they are using the correct verb forms and colour words.

ANSWERS
Students' own answers.

> **Extra activity: *Kim's game***
> - On a tray, place a selection of the classroom objects from exercise 4. Alternatively, you can write the names of the objects on the board and rub them off.
> - In groups, students have two minutes to memorize what is on the tray or board.
> - Remove an object and ask students to write down which object has been removed. Continue until the tray or board is empty.
> - Check the answers with the class. The group with all the objects in the correct order is the winner.

Time page 6

Aim

To review the time

Warm-up

- Ask students what the day, date, and time is.

Exercise 1 08

- Look at the clock face and go through the times as a class.
- If it is helpful, copy the clock face onto the board.
- Play the CD. Students listen and repeat chorally, then individually.

Transcript Student's Book page 6

Extra activity

- Draw a clock on the board and point to different times asking students to say what time it is.
- Draw blank clock faces on the board with the times written below each one and ask students to come out and draw the hands in the correct place.

Exercise 2

- Students write the times below the clocks.
- They can compare answers in pairs.
- Check the answers with the class.

ANSWERS

2 ten to three   3 twenty past seven
4 ten past ten   5 quarter to eight   6 five past five
7 twenty-five past four   8 half past three

Exercise 3 09

- Play the CD. Students listen and write the times.
- Check the answers with the class.
- Students listen again and repeat chorally, then individually.

ANSWERS / AUDIO CD TRACK 09

1 It's three o'clock.
2 It's half past four.
3 It's quarter past eleven.
4 It's quarter to ten.
5 It's twenty to one.
6 It's ten to eight.
7 It's twenty-five past one.
8 It's five to five.

Exercise 4 Pairwork

- In pairs, students ask and answer about the clocks in exercise 2.
- Monitor and check that students are using the singular form of *be* in the question and answer, and remind them to swap roles.

ANSWERS

Students' own answers.

Days, months, and seasons page 7

Aim

To review days of the week and months of the year; to ask and answer about birthdays; to review the four seasons

Warm-up

- Ask students what day it is today, what day it was yesterday, what day it is tomorrow, and what month it is.

Exercise 1

- Students complete the puzzle individually.
- They can compare answers in pairs.
- Check the answers with the class.

ANSWERS

1 Thursday   2 Tuesday   3 Wednesday   4 Saturday
5 Monday

Exercise 2 10

- Students write the days of the week in the correct order.
- Play the CD. Students listen and check.
- Students listen again and repeat chorally, then individually.

ANSWERS / AUDIO CD TRACK 10

1 Sunday   2 Monday   3 Tuesday   4 Wednesday
5 Thursday   6 Friday   7 Saturday

Exercise 3 11

- Students, individually or in pairs, write the months in the box in the correct order.
- Play the CD. Students listen and check.
- Students listen again and repeat chorally, then individually.

ANSWERS / AUDIO CD TRACK 11

January   February   March   April   May   June   July
August   September   October   November   December

Extra activity

- Call out a day of the week or a month of the year for students to say the next day or month, e.g. T: *Monday* SS: *Tuesday*.

Exercise 4 ⊙ 12

- Play the CD. Students listen and read.
- Students listen again and repeat chorally.

Transcript Student's Book page 7

- In pairs, students ask and answer which month their birthday is. Monitor for correct pronunciation.
- Ask for class feedback and find out which is the most common month for birthdays in the class.

ANSWERS
Students' own answers.

Exercise 5

- Ask students how many seasons there are (four) and write the word *season* on the board. Ask which season we are in now and what the next season will be.
- Students match the names of the seasons in the box with the pictures.
- Check the answers with the class.

ANSWERS
1 spring 2 summer 3 autumn 4 winter

Introductions page 8

Aim

To review introductions

Warm-up

- Give a brief introduction to the photo story. Tell them that the teenagers are all students at a stage school in Britain (a school which specializes in the performing arts). Explain that one of the teenagers is a new student at the school.
- Ask the students how they would introduce themselves in English to someone when they meet them for the first time.

Exercise 1

- Ask the students to look at the picture. Ask different students to read out the speech bubbles.

Exercise 2 Focus on you

- Students complete the dialogue with their names.
- They practise reading the dialogue in pairs.
- Go through the box. Check the students' comprehension of each of the subject pronouns and practise their pronunciation.

Exercise 3

- Check that the students understand the activity. Ask them to look at the different forms of *be* in the sentences. Point out the short form in the example and ask them to use the short forms in each sentence.
- The students rewrite the sentences using subject pronouns.
- They can compare answers in pairs.
- Check the answers with the class.

ANSWERS
1 They're friends.
2 It's a capital city.
3 We're students.

4 He's in my class.
5 She's a fantastic singer.
6 You're students.

be: present simple page 8

Aims

To review the meaning and use of the verb *be* in its present simple form; to use the verb *be* in introductions

Warm-up

- Books closed, on the board write gapped versions of the different forms of *be* in the present simple.
- Ask students to come to the board and complete them.
- Books open again, go through the box and check the meaning and pronunciation of the full and short forms.

Exercise 4

- Students circle the correct verbs.
- Check the answers with the class.

ANSWERS
1 is 2 is 3 are 4 are 5 are 6 am

Exercise 5

- Students rewrite the sentences in exercise 4 with short forms.
- Check the answers with the class.

ANSWERS
1 It's black.
2 He's Simon.
3 We're students.
4 They're teachers.
5 You're in my class.
6 I'm English.

Extra activity

- Write the subject pronouns *I*, *he*, *she*, *we*, and *they* on the board. Explain that students are going to introduce themselves and their classmates to you. They must use the subject pronoun you point to and give corresponding names of pupils in the class. As an example start with *I* and give your name: *I'm Ana Maria*. Go round the class asking individual students to do the introductions.

Possessive adjectives page 9

Aim

To review the meanings and correct usage of possessive adjectives

Warm-up

- Ask students to look at the photos. Ask them where the people are and what they're doing (They're at school and they're introducing themselves).

Exercise 1

- Students read through the dialogue in pairs and find two mistakes.

> **ANSWER**
> Her name is Holly, not Polly.
> Edinburgh is the capital of Scotland, not England.

- Ask students who the new student in the photo story is (Holly).
- Go through the box with the students. Check the meaning and pronunciation of the subject pronouns and possessive adjectives.

Exercise 2

- In pairs, students read the sentences carefully and circle either a subject pronoun or a possessive adjective in each sentence.
- Check the answers with the class, making sure students understand all the new vocabulary.

> **ANSWERS**
> 1 My 2 They 3 Her 4 Its 5 He 6 Your 7 Our

Exercise 3

- Remind students that possessive adjectives link to the person or object they are referring to, not what they possess. Write an example on the board:
  Jack's shoes: His shoes ✓ *Their shoes* ✗
- Students look at the pictures and complete the sentences with *his*, *her*, or *its*.
- Check the answers with the class, making sure students understand all the new vocabulary.

> **ANSWERS**
> 1 his 2 Its 3 his 4 her 5 her

Exercise 4

- Students complete the sentences individually with the correct possessive adjectives.
- They can compare answers in pairs.
- Check the answers with the class, making sure students understand all the new vocabulary.

> **ANSWERS**
> 1 Her 2 His 3 My; your 4 Our 5 its 6 Your
> 7 Their 8 her

> ### Extra activity
> - Looking at the sentences from exercise 4, students write a short text about themselves and their families. They should use as many possessive adjectives as they can.

Countries and nationalities page 10

Aims

To review different countries and nationalities from around the world; to practise talking about your country of origin and nationality

Warm-up

- Ask students if they have travelled abroad to another country, if they have relatives in another country, or if there's a country they would like to visit. Elicit the different countries and write them on the board. Ask the class what they know about the country, e.g. which continent it's in, its capital, what language is spoken there. Practise the pronunciation of each of the country names.

Exercise 1 13

- Tell the students to look at the map. Tell them they are going to match as many numbers to countries as they can. Explain that they don't have to match them all – they will find out the names of all the countries soon.
- In pairs, students match the numbers with the countries.
- Play the CD. Students listen and check.
- Students listen again and repeat each country chorally, then individually.

> **ANSWERS / AUDIO CD TRACK 13**
> 1 Canada 2 the United Kingdom (the UK) 3 Russia
> 4 the United States (the US) 5 Spain 6 Greece
> 7 China 8 South Korea 9 Japan 10 Mexico
> 11 Vietnam 12 Chile 13 Argentina 14 South Africa
> 15 Australia

> ### Extra activity
> - In pairs, students take turns to cover the names of the countries on the map and to try and remember their names. The other student says if they have got the correct answer.

Exercise 2 14

- Students work individually to match the countries from exercise 1 with their nationalities.
- Play the CD. Students listen and check.
- Students listen again and repeat chorally, then individually.

> **ANSWERS**
> 1 the United States (the US) 2 Vietnam 3 Russia
> 4 Canada 5 Japan 6 South Africa 7 China
> 8 Mexico 9 the United Kingdom (the UK) 10 Greece
> 11 Spain 12 South Korea 13 Australia 14 Chile

Exercise 3

- Students write the nationalities in the correct columns.

> **ANSWERS**
> 1 Russian 2 Australian 3 Argentinian 4 Chilean
> 5 American 6 South African 7 Mexican 8 South
> Korean 9 Vietnamese 10 Japanese 11 Chinese
> 12 British 13 Spanish 14 Greek

Exercise 4 Pairwork

- Refer students back to exercise 1. In pairs, they take turns to pick a country. They make dialogues asking and answering about their country of origin and nationality.
- Check that students are using the correct form of *be* and the correct ending for each nationality in their questions and answers. Remind them to swap roles.

Students' own answers.

Singulars and plurals   page 11

Aims

To review the use of *a / an*; to practise the correct spelling of regular and irregular plural forms

Warm-up

- On the board write four nouns beginning with a consonant and four beginning with a vowel, e.g. *man, table, watch, city, orange, answer, apple, exercise*. Mix them up so that the difference between the two sets is less clear. Draw two columns below. Write *a* at the top of one and *an* at the top of the other. Ask individual students to come to the board and write the nouns in the correct column.
- Ask the whole class when we use *a* and *an*. Elicit their responses and write the answer on the board: *a* precedes a noun starting with a consonant and *an* precedes a noun starting with a vowel. Point out that their use makes pronunciation easier, e.g. *a exercise* would be difficult to pronounce. Don't wipe the nouns off the board.

Exercise 1

- Students complete the spaces with *a* or *an*.
- Check the answers with the class, making sure students understand all the new vocabulary.

1 a   2 an   3 an   4 a   5 an   6 an   7 a   8 a

Exercise 2

- Refer students back to the nouns on the board from the warm-up activity.
- Ask individual students to guess how they are spelt in their plural forms.
- Write the plural forms of the nouns on the board and practise their pronunciation with the class.
- Point out that the plural nouns are examples of the four different plural forms.
- The students complete the table with the plural forms of the nouns.
- Check the answers with the class, making sure students understand all the new vocabulary. Practise the pronunciation of the plural forms with the class. Point out that in the plural form of nouns ending in *ss, sh, s,* and *ch, es* is pronounced /ɪz/.

1 ice creams   2 rubbers   3 books   4 boxes   5 buses
6 sandwiches   7 classes   8 tomatoes   9 babies
10 families   11 countries   12 men   13 women
14 children   15 people

there is / there are   page 11

Aim

To review the meaning and use of *there is / there are*

Warm-up

- Check the meanings of *there is* and *there are*.
- Point to a classroom object and make a sentence about it with *there is*, e.g. *There's a book.* Do the same with two of the same object, e.g. *There are two pencils.*

Exercise 3

- Ask students to look at the pictures and count how many of each object there are. Refer them back to exercise 2, where they will find most of the necessary vocabulary.
- Point out the short form *there's* in the example. Ask students to use it in the appropriate answers.
- Students complete the sentences with *there's / there are*, and the correct number and noun.
- They can compare answers in pairs.
- Check the answers with the class.

1 There are four buses.
2 There are seven boxes.
3 There's an ice cream.
4 There's a family. / There are three people.
5 There are five ice creams.
6 There are two women. / There are two people.
7 There are three babies.
8 There are two children.
9 There are four kites.

Extra activity 1

- In pairs, students practise making sentences with *there is / there are* and classroom objects.

Extra activity 2

- Ask the students to close their books.
- Play *Hangman* to practise the plural form of the nouns used in exercise 2.
- Divide the class into two teams.
- Write the gapped versions of the plural nouns on the board. Ask students to call out letters and complete a hangman frame if they do not guess the correct letter. The team with the most correct answers wins.

---

1 Is she your friend?

Grammar
be: present simple (negative, interrogative and short answers)
Question words (*Who, What, Where, When, How old*)
this, that, these, those

Vocabulary
Adjectives

Communication
Asking and answering personal questions
Falling intonation in *Wh-* questions

Skills
Reading: The Star Academy staff
Listening: An interview with a teacher
Speaking: Role play an interview
Writing: A personal profile

Topics
Society: School and education

Presentation page 12

Aim
To present the new language in a motivating context

Story
Holly and Luke are getting to know each other better. They both see a poster for auditions for a new musical. Ruby arrives and is not happy that Holly is considering going for an audition.

Warm-up
• Write the following questions on the board:
  How many students are there? Who are they?
  Where are they? What is on the wall?
• Focus on the photo of the characters and in the students' L1, ask how many students there are in the photo (three), who they are (Holly, Luke, and Ruby), where they are (at school), and what is on the wall (a poster about auditions for a school musical).
• Pre-teach *poster*, *musical*, and *audition*.
• Ask students to match the questions you have just asked to the questions on the board.

Exercise 1 Read and listen 🔘 15
• Explain that students must listen to find out Holly's surname. Check they understand the meaning of *surname*.
• Play the CD. Students listen and read.
• Check the answer with the class.

• Draw students' attention to the *Check it out!* box and make sure students understand the expressions in the text.
• Go through any other unknown vocabulary in the text.
• Students listen again and repeat chorally, then individually.

ANSWER
b Wood

Transcript   Student's Book page 12

Exercise 2 Comprehension
• Students match the sentence halves individually.
• They can look back at the dialogue in exercise 1.
• Check the answers with the class.

ANSWERS
1 b   2 c   3 a

Extra activity
• Students can act out the dialogue in groups of three.

Consolidation
• Remind students to copy any new words or phrases into their vocabulary books.

Language focus page 13

Aim
To practise the target language in a new context

Exercise 3 Dialogue focus
• Remind students that they are using language from exercise 1 in this activity.
• Students complete the dialogues with the questions in the box. Encourage them to use the photos to help them work out the context and to look back at exercise 1 if necessary.
• They can compare answers in pairs.
• Do not check answers at this point.

Exercise 4 🔘 16
• Play the CD. Students listen and check their answers to exercise 3.
• Students listen again and repeat chorally, then individually.

ANSWERS / AUDIO CD TRACK 16
1 **Luke** How old are you, Holly?
  Holly I'm thirteen.
  Luke [1]What's your surname, Holly?
  Holly It's Wood.
2 **Holly** Look! [2]Is that Ruby?
  Luke Yes, it is.
3 **Holly** [3]Is she your friend?
  Luke No, she isn't.
4 **Luke** [4]What's this?
  Ruby It's a poster, Luke!

Exercise 5 Focus on you

- Students complete the dialogue with information about themselves.
- Remind them to look back at exercise 3 if necessary.
- Monitor and check students are using the correct question words and make a note of any repeated errors to check at the end of the lesson.

ANSWERS
Students' own answers.

Exercise 6 Pairwork

- In pairs, students practise the dialogue they completed in exercise 5.

Extra activity

- Ask one or two pairs to act out their dialogues for the class.

Vocabulary page 14

Adjectives

Aim

To present and practise some opinion adjectives: *boring, difficult, easy, fantastic, funny, interesting, serious, terrible*

Warm-up

- Write the adjectives on the board and ask students if any of them are similar in their language.
- Check their meanings.

Exercise 1 ⊚ 17

- Students choose the correct adjective to describe each picture.
- They can compare answers in pairs.
- Play the CD. Students listen and check their answers.
- Students listen again and repeat chorally, then individually.

ANSWERS / AUDIO CD TRACK 17
1 It's interesting.
2 It's boring.
3 She's terrible.
4 She's fantastic.
5 It's easy.
6 It's difficult.
7 He's funny.
8 He's serious.

Exercise 2 Pairwork

- In pairs, students give their opinions on the people and things in the photos.
- Draw students' attention to the *Look!* box and remind them that adjectives do not change form in English.
- Monitor and check students are using adjectives correctly and make a note of any repeated errors to check at the end of the lesson.
- Ask for pairs to give their views to the class.

ANSWERS
Students' own answers.

Background notes

- *Harry Potter* is a series of seven fantasy novels written by J K Rowling. The first book was published in 1997 and tells the story of the young wizard, Harry Potter, and his friends Ron Weasley and Hermione Granger at the Hogwarts School of Witchcraft and Wizardry. The books were made into a series of highly successful films starring Daniel Radcliffe as Harry Potter.
- Ozzy Osbourne is an English singer and songwriter. He used to sing with the heavy metal band *Black Sabbath*. He has become a reality TV star in a programme about his own family called *The Osbournes*. His wife and manager, Sharon, and two of his children, Jack and Kelly, also starred in the programme.
- Lady Gaga is an American singer and songwriter. Her real name is Stefani Germanotta and she was born in New York. She became famous in 2008 when she released her debut album, *The Fame*. She has won a lot of awards for her work.
- *Shrek the Third* is the third film in the Shrek series produced by DreamWorks Animation. The films tell the story of the ogre Shrek and his wife Fiona, and their faithful companion, Donkey. Mike Myers is the voice of Shrek, Cameron Diaz is Princess Fiona, and Eddie Murphy is the voice of Donkey.
- Jack Sparrow is a character from the *Pirates of the Caribbean* films. He may have been based on a real pirate called Bartholomew Roberts who lived in the 18th century. In the films, Jack Sparrow is played by the actor, Johnny Depp.
- Ben Stiller is an American comedian and actor from New York. He is best known for his roles as the museum guard, Larry Daley, in *Night at the Museum 1* and *2*.
- Cristiano Ronaldo is a Portuguese football player who was born on the island of Madeira. He played football for Manchester United from 2003 to 2009. He then moved to Real Madrid. He has won the prestigious *FIFA World Player of the Year* award and is said to be one of the world's greatest football players.

Extra activity

- Give students the names of other TV, film, pop, and sports stars and ask for their opinion of them.

Consolidation

- Encourage students to copy the adjectives into their vocabulary notebooks. They can put these in alphabetical order, use a mind map, or record them with the translations in a different colour.

Further practice
CD-ROM; Workbook page 71

Grammar page 15

be: present simple (Negative)

Aim

To present and practise the negative form of *be:* present simple

Warm-up

* Write two incorrect sentences about Holly on the board: *Holly is twelve. Holly is in Year 8.* Ask students why the sentences are wrong. Next to the sentences write *Holly ___ twelve. She ___ thirteen. Holly _____ Year 8. She _____ Year 9.*

* See if students can complete the sentences. If not, do it for them, perhaps with the forms of *be* in a different colour. Tell students they are going to learn the negative form of *be*.

Grammar box

* Go through the grammar box with the class, drawing students' attention to the short forms. Check the meaning of the different forms and practise the pronunciation of the long and short forms. Remind students that verbs must always be preceded by a subject pronoun in English.

* Ask students to look back at the dialogue on page 12 and to find more examples.

Exercise 1

* Students transform the affirmative sentences into negative.

* They can compare answers in pairs.

* Check the answers with the class.

ANSWERS

1 I'm not English.
2 You aren't in my class.
3 Mr Allen isn't American.
4 We aren't actors.
5 They aren't from London.
6 It isn't a new computer.

Extra activity

* Call out the affirmative form of the verb *be* for students to say the negative form, e.g. T: *I am*   SS: *I'm not*, etc.

Exercise 2

* Students complete the sentences with *'m not, isn't*, or *aren't.*

* They can compare answers in pairs.

* Check the answers with the class.

ANSWERS

1 I'm not American.
2 She isn't fourteen.
3 He isn't my brother.
4 You aren't in England.
5 We aren't at the cinema.
6 They aren't teachers.

Extra activity

* In small groups, students choose a character from exercise 2 on page 14. They say the sentence and the other students must guess who they are, e.g. SS 1: *I'm not serious.*   SS 2: *You're Ben Stiller.*

Interrogative and short answers

Aim

To present and practise the interrogative and short answer forms of *be:* present simple

Warm-up

* Write a few affirmative sentences with *be* on the board, e.g. *Luke and Holly are friends. The Star Academy is a school.* Show how questions are made with the present simple form of *be* by rubbing out the verb in the sentences and putting it at the beginning to make questions: *Are Luke and Holly friends? Is the Star Academy a school?*

* Go round the class asking students simple questions with *be*, e.g. *Are you thirteen? Is his name Mario? Am I the teacher?* They should answer *Yes* or *No* to show that they have understood.

Grammar box

* Go through the grammar box with the class.

* Practise the pronunciation.

Rules page 70

Exercise 3

* Individually, students write questions and answers using *be:* present simple.

* They can compare answers in pairs.

* Check the answers with the class.

ANSWERS

1 Is she thirteen today? No, she isn't.
2 Are they at school? No, they aren't.
3 Is it easy? No, it isn't.
4 Is she a teacher? Yes, she is.
5 Are you and your friend ten? No, we aren't.
6 Is he a famous actor? Yes, he is.

Finished?

* Students write five questions for a partner to answer.

* In pairs, they ask and answer their questions.

* Ask one or two pairs to ask and answer in front of the class.

ANSWERS

Students' own answers.

Extra activity

* In small groups, one student thinks of a famous person. The others must ask questions using *be:* present simple to guess who it is. Students can have a maximum of ten questions, e.g. SS 2: *Are you funny?*   SS 1: *No, I'm not.* SS 3: *Are you a film star?*   SS 1: *Yes, I am.*, etc.

* Before the activity begins, pre-teach some useful vocabulary, e.g. *actor, novel, singer, film, comedian, football player.*

Consolidation

* Encourage students to copy the grammar rules and examples into their grammar notebooks.

| Further practice
| CD-ROM; Workbook page 71

Communication page 16

Asking and answering personal questions

Aim
To present and practise giving information about your name, surname, age, address, phone number, email address

Warm-up
- On the board write the following words, one below the other: *name*, *surname*, *age*.
- Ask students if they can remember this information about the new girl in the photo story (Holly).
- Ask students to complete her personal details.
- Focus on the photo and ask students if they can guess where Jack is (at a gym).
- Ask the students why Jack might have to give personal information at a gym (Possible answer: He is joining as a member).

Exercise 1 ⊚ 18
- Students listen and complete the dialogue with the questions in the box.
- Encourage them to look at the answers to find which question they need.
- Play the CD again. Students listen and check their answers.
- Students listen again and repeat.

ANSWERS / AUDIO CD TRACK 18
Receptionist What's your first name?
Jack It's Jack.
Receptionist ¹What's your surname?
Jack It's Wells.
Receptionist W-E-L-L-S? Is that correct?
Jack Yes, it is.
Receptionist ²How old are you, Jack?
Jack I'm fourteen.
Receptionist ³What's your address?
Jack It's 12, West Street, London, NW3 4EA.
Receptionist ⁴What's your phone number?
Jack It's 020 7946 0787 and my mobile number is 07700 900321.
Receptionist ⁵What's your email address?
Jack It's jackw@freesurf.com

You ask, You answer
- Go through the *You ask, You answer* box with the class. Practise the pronunciation of the words in the questions with the class.
- In pairs, students ask and answer questions using the information in the box.

Exercise 2 Pronunciation ⊚ 19
- Read the questions in the box, showing students how the intonation in information questions in English falls.
- Play the CD. Students listen and read.
- Students listen again and repeat chorally, then individually.

Transcript Student's Book page 16

Extra activity
- If students need more practice, read the questions from exercise 2 starting from the end for students to repeat chorally, then individually, e.g. *name?*, *first name?*, *your first name?*, *What's your first name?*

Exercise 3 Pairwork
- Students take turns to ask and answer the questions in exercise 1.
- Monitor for correct pronunciation and intonation.
- Ask one or two pairs to ask and answer in front of the class.

ANSWERS
Students' own answers.

Extra activity
- In pairs, students cover the *You ask* section of the box in exercise 1 and take turns to ask and answer questions about the information.
- Check that students are taking turns to ask and answer and that they are using the correct pronunciation and intonation. Make a note of any repeated errors to check at the end of the lesson.

Further practice
CD-ROM; Workbook page 73

Grammar page 17

Question words

Aim
To present and practise question words

Warm-up
- Ask students one or two questions, e.g. *What's your name? What's your surname? How old are you?*
- Write the question words from the questions on the board and check their meanings.

Grammar box
- Go through the grammar box with the class. Draw students' attention to the word order in questions and the short forms.
- Ask students to look back at the dialogue on page 12 and to find more examples.
- Practise the pronunciation and intonation of the questions.

Rules page 70

Exercise 1
- Students match the questions (1–5) with the answers (a–e) individually.
- They can compare answers in pairs.
- Check the answers with the class.

ANSWERS
2 c   3 e   4 b   5 a

> **Extra activity**
> - In pairs, students ask and answer the questions in exercise 1 about themselves.

Exercise 2
- Students complete the questions with the correct question words individually.
- Encourage them to look at the answers to the questions before they choose the word.
- They can compare answers in pairs.
- Check the answers with the class.

ANSWERS
1 Who   2 Where   3 When   4 How old   5 What

> **Extra activity**
> - Give students a few minutes to look at the questions and their answers in exercise 2.
> - Books closed. Call out an answer and ask students to give you the appropriate question. Alternatively, you can do this with different questions and answers.

Exercise 3 Game!
- In pairs, students play an asking and answering game.
- Monitor and check students are using questions forms correctly and make a note of any repeated errors to check at the end.

> **Consolidation**
> - Remind students to copy the grammar rules and examples into their grammar notebooks..

this, that, these, those

Aim
To present and practise *this, that, these,* and *those*

Warm-up
- Pick up a few objects on your desk and point to some objects further away from you and ask *What's this? What's that? What are these? What are those?* Write *this, that, these,* and *those* on the board and elicit their meanings.
- Go through the grammar box with the class.
- Make sure students understand the difference between the words (*this, these* for objects near you and *that, those* for objects further away from you).
- Practise the pronunciation of the sentences in the box.

Rules page 70

Exercise 4
- Students complete the sentences individually with *this, that, these,* or *those*.
- They can compare answers in pairs.
- Check the answers with the class.

ANSWERS
1 Those are my friends.
2 This is my new mobile phone.
3 These are your books.
4 'Who's that?' 'She's our maths teacher.'

Exercise 5 Pairwork
- As in the warm-up, demonstrate *What's this? What's that? What are these? What are those?* by pointing to objects near and further away from you and asking the questions.
- Elicit the students' answers.
- In pairs, students continue the activity.
- Check students are taking turns to ask and answer, and monitor for correct pronunciation and intonation. Make a note of any repeated errors to check at the end of the lesson.

Finished?
- Students write their own questions for you, using question words.

ANSWERS
Students' own questions and teacher's own answers.

> **Extra activity**
> - Pick up or point to different classroom objects for students to respond using a demonstrative, e.g.
> - *T: (holding up a pencil) SS: this*, etc.

| Further practice
CD-ROM; Workbook page 72

Skills Pages 18–19

Reading

Aim

To read and understand personal information in a school newsletter

Warm-up

- Ask students *Who are the people in the photos?* (people who work at *Star Academy*)
- Remind students of the adjectives they have learned in the unit that could describe the people and write them on the board.
- Ask them to make sentences about the people using the adjectives, e.g. *I think Mandy Parkinson is funny*.
- Elicit / Pre-teach school subjects. Ask students to find two examples of school subjects in the text (drama and music).

Exercise 1

- Students read the texts silently.
- Check any unknown vocabulary with the class.
- Students answer the questions. Remind them to write full answers.
- Students can compare answers in pairs.
- Check the answers with the class.

ANSWERS
1 The music teacher is Barbara Linton.
2 She's from Cardiff, Wales.
3 His first name is Arthur.
4 His favourite musicals are *The Lion King* and *Mamma Mia!*
5 She's from Bristol.
6 Her passion is Latin American dancing.

Extra activity

- Ask students more questions about the people in the text, e.g. *Who is the head teacher at Star Academy?* (John Lane) *What is his favourite opera?* (The Barber of Seville), etc.

Listening

Aim

To listen to and understand information in an interview with a teacher

Warm-up

- Check students know the meaning of *geography*.

Exercise 2 ⊙ 20

- Before beginning the activity, check students understand the sentences in the exercise and encourage them to look for key words in each item to listen for.
- Play the CD. Students listen and choose the correct answers.
- Check the answers with the class.

ANSWERS / AUDIO CD TRACK 20

1 a 2 b 3 b 4 a 5 a

Student Mrs Henderson. What's your first name?
Mrs Henderson My name's Emma Henderson.
Student Where are you from, Mrs Henderson?
Mrs Henderson I'm from Leeds, in the north of England.
Student How old are you?
Mrs Henderson Erm… I'm 34.
Student What are your hobbies?
Mrs Henderson My passions are music and the cinema.
Student Who's your favourite singer?
Mrs Henderson My favourite singer is Enrique Iglesias. He's Spanish. He's a great singer.
Student What's your favourite film?
Mrs Henderson My favourite film is an American film. It's *Toy Story*. It's fantastic!

Speaking

Aim

To ask and answer about personal information

Warm-up

- Ask students what they can remember about Holly.

Exercise 3

- Revise the verb *be* in the present simple, including its short forms, and possessive adjectives with the class.
- Students read Holly's factfile and complete the interview.
- Remind them to use the short form of *be* in their questions and answers.
- Check the answers with the class.

ANSWERS

1 name's Holly Wood 2 are you from 3 Scotland
4 How old are you 5 your favourite singer
6 singer's Lily Allen

Exercise 4 Pairwork

- In pairs, students practise the dialogue in exercise 3.
- Remind them to swap roles. Monitor and help as necessary, making a note of any repeated errors to check at the end of the lesson.

Writing

Aim

To write a description of Holly

Exercise 5

- Students read Holly's description, and find and correct the mistakes.
- They can compare answers in pairs.
- Check the answers with the class.
- You can write the description on the board and ask volunteers to make the corrections on the board.

ANSWERS

1 Her surname isn't Good, it's Wood.
2 She isn't twelve years old, she's thirteen.
3 She isn't from Wales, she's from Scotland.
4 Her favourite singer isn't Shakira, it's Lily Allen.

Exercise 6

- Students use Holly's text as a model and write the correct description.
- Students write a rough draft first and swap with a partner, who corrects it.
- Students write a final version, making sure they have corrected any errors.

Extra activity
- Students can write their own factfiles about themselves, without putting their name.
- Collect them in and give them out for others to guess who it is.

Consolidation
- Remind students to make a note of any new words or phrases from the lesson in their vocabulary books.

Further practice
CD-ROM; Workbook page 73

# Have you got a mobile phone?

Grammar

have got: present simple (affirmative and negative)

have got: present simple (interrogative and short answers)

Possessive *'s*

Vocabulary

The family

Communication

Talking about possessions

/h/

Skills

Reading: The perfect celebrity family

Listening: Jack's family

Speaking: Describe *The Simpsons* family

Writing: Celebrity family

Topics

Society: Family life and its importance

Presentation page 20

Aim

To present the new language in a motivating context

Story

Luke gives Holly the phone number of the drama teacher and encourages her to call about the auditions. Ruby arrives and tells Holly that Mr Smith, the drama teacher, is her uncle. Holly feels she will never be able to compete with Ruby to get the part.

Warm-up

- Ask students what they can remember from the last part of the photo story.
- Ask students to look at the photos of the characters and ask a few questions: *Who is in the photo?* (Holly, Luke, and Ruby) *Are they in a lesson?* (No) Explain that they are in the school common room, a room where students can relax between lessons. *What is in the room?* (Posters, sofas, cups) *What is Holly doing?* (Holly is thinking about making a telephone call).

Exercise 1 Read and listen 21

- Pre-teach the word *uncle*.
- Play the CD. Students read and listen to find out who Ruby's uncle is.
- Remind students they don't have to understand every word. Play the CD again if necessary.
- Check the answer with the class.

- Check students have understood the dialogue, refer them to the *Check it out!* box and explain the phrases.
- Students listen again and repeat chorally, then individually.

ANSWER

The drama teacher, Mr Smith.

Transcript Student's Book page 20

Exercise 2 Comprehension

- Students complete the exercise individually.
- Check the answers with the class.

ANSWERS

1 True.   2 False. Mr Smith is Ruby's uncle.   3 False. Ruby doesn't like Holly.

> **Extra activity**
> - In groups of three, students act out the dialogue.

Language focus page 21

Aim

To practise the target language in a new context

Exercise 3 Dialogue focus

- Students complete the dialogues with the questions in the box. Encourage them to look at the photos to help them work out the answers.
- They can compare answers in pairs. Do not check the answers at this point.

Exercise 4 22

- Play the CD. Students listen and check their answers to exercise 3.
- Students listen again and repeat chorally, then individually.

ANSWERS / AUDIO CD TRACK 22

1

Luke Where's your mobile phone?

Holly I haven't got a mobile phone.

2

Holly Have you got a mobile phone?

Luke Yes, I have. Here you are.

3

Holly What's Mr Smith's phone number?

Luke It's 416 ...

4

Holly What? Is that true, Luke?

Luke Yes, it is. Mr Smith is Ruby's uncle.

> **Extra activity**
> - In groups of three, students act out the dialogues.
> - Encourage them to do it without looking at their books.

Exercise 5 Focus on you

- Students number the sentences in the correct order to make a conversation.

ANSWERS

1 Have you got a mobile phone?
2 Yes, I have.
3 What's your number?
4 It's 0717 … .
5 Thanks.

Exercise 6 Pairwork

- In pairs, students practise the conversation in exercise 5.
- Remind them to swap roles.
- Ask one or two pairs to act out their dialogues for the class.

> ### Consolidation
> - Remind students to copy any new vocabulary into their vocabulary notebooks.

Vocabulary page 22

The family

Aim

To present and practise family vocabulary: *aunt*, *brother*, *cousin*, *dad*, *grandad*, *grandma*, *grandparents*, *mum*, *parents*, *sister*, *uncle*

Warm-up

- Ask students if they have ever seen their own family tree.
- Ask a student to come out and draw their family tree on the board. Encourage students to add any family words in English if they can.
- Ask students if they have brothers or sisters and how many they have.

Exercise 1 23

- Books closed, pre-teach the target vocabulary and practise its pronunciation. Don't leave any translations on the board.
- Books open, students complete Ruby's family tree with the words in the box.
- They can compare answers in pairs.
- Play the CD. Students listen and check their answers.
- Students listen again and repeat chorally, then individually.

ANSWERS / AUDIO CD TRACK 23

This is my family.
This is Edward. He's my grandad.
This is Tilly. She's my [1]grandma.
They're my [2]grandparents.
This is Arthur. He's my [3]uncle.
This is Helen. She's my [4]aunt.
This is Fiona. She's my [5]mum.
And this is James. He's my [6]dad.
They're my [7]parents.
This is Thomas. He's my [8]cousin.
This is me!
And these are Megan and Ben.
She's my [9]sister and he's my [10]brother.

Exercise 2

- Students complete the exercise individually or in pairs. Remind them to refer back to the family tree in exercise 1 if necessary.
- Check the answers with the class.

ANSWERS

1 sister 2 mum 3 parents 4 cousin 5 aunt
6 uncle 7 brother

> ### Extra activity
> - Students look at Ruby's family tree for a few minutes and try to remember all the members of her family.
> - Books closed. Call out the names of different members in Ruby's family for students to tell you who they are, e.g. T: *Who's Tilly?* SS: *Ruby's grandma.* This can be done as a whole class or small group activity.

Exercise 3 Pairwork

- Students write the names of five people in their families and give their list to a partner.
- In pairs, students ask and answer about each other's family. Remind them to swap roles.
- Monitor and check students are using the correct question and the correct family words, and make a note of any repeated errors to check at the end of the lesson.

ANSWERS
Students' own answers.

> ### Extra activity
> - Students draw their own family tree using Ruby's as a model. This can be done for homework and students can add photos.
> - The family trees can be displayed in the classroom.

> ### Consolidation
> - Remind students to copy any new vocabulary into their vocabulary notebooks.

Further practice
CD-ROM; Workbook page 76

Grammar page 23

have got: present simple (Affirmative)

Aim

To present and practise *have got*: present simple (affirmative)

Warm-up

- Write a gapped version of *have got* without vowels on the board and ask students if they can complete the words.
- Explain the meaning of the verb.

Grammar box

- Go through the grammar box with the class.
- Explain when we use the short forms of *have got* (in spoken and informal written English).
- Practise the pronunciation of the different forms.
- Ask the students to find examples of *have got* affirmative in the photo story on page 20.

Exercise 1

- Students complete the sentences with *have got* or *has got*.
- They can compare answers in pairs.
- Check the answers with the class.

ANSWERS

1	have got	4	have got
2	has got	5	have got
3	have got	6	has got

Exercise 2

- Students rewrite the sentences from exercise 1 with the short forms *'ve got* and *'s got*.
- Check the answers with the class.

ANSWERS

1	You've got	4	I've got
2	She's got	5	We've got
3	They've got	6	He's got

> **Extra activity**
> - Call out subject pronouns and objects and ask individual students to make sentences, e.g.
>   T: *I / computer* SS: *I've got a computer.*
>   T: *he / mobile phone* SS: *He's got a mobile phone.*

Exercise 3 Game!

- Students play a memory game in groups.
- Split the class into groups of about ten students.
- One student begins by making a sentence with *I've got* ...
- The student sitting on his or her left repeats the first sentence but with *He's got* or *She's got* ... .The student then makes a sentence of their own with *I've got*. The third student must remember the first two sentences and construct them in the third person before making a sentence of their own. The game continues until one student forgets one of the sentences and is out of the game. The last student in the game is the winner.

have got: present simple (Negative)

Aim

To present and practise *have got*: present simple (negative)

Warm-up

- Play *Hangman* (see Teacher's Book page 9) to present the negative form of *have got*.
  Ask students to look again at the photo story on page 20 and to find examples of the negative forms of *have got*.

Grammar box

- Go through the grammar box and practise the pronunciation of the long and short forms.

Exercise 4

- Students make the sentences negative using short forms.
- They can compare answers in pairs.
- Check the answers with the class.

ANSWERS
1 We haven't got a DVD player.
2 I haven't got a pen in my rucksack.
3 She hasn't got a big family.
4 They haven't got a good music teacher.

Exercise 5

- Check that students know what all the objects in the table are and that they understand the activity.
- Remind them to be careful which form of *have got* they choose.
- In pairs, students look at the ticks and crosses in the table and write sentences using the prompts.
- Check the answers with the class.

ANSWERS
1 Rebecca has got a digital camera.
2 David hasn't got an MP3 player.
3 Rebecca and David haven't got a games console.
4 David has got a digital camera.
5 Tom and Rebecca have got an MP3 player.

Finished?

- Students use the sentences in exercise 5 to write their own true sentences about their possessions. They can use different objects, too.

> **Extra activity: *Chinese Whispers***
> - Put students in groups of ten. Write down sentences with the affirmative and negative forms of *have got* on pieces of paper. Give a sentence to one person in each group and ask them to read it, but not show it to anyone else in the group. The student then whispers the sentence to the person on their left. The game continues until the last student whispers the sentence in the first student's ear. The first student then tells the whole group what he or she heard and shows the group the original sentence.

▮ Further practice
CD-ROM; Workbook page 76

Communication page 24

Talking about possessions

Aim

To ask and answer about personal possessions

Warm-up

- Go round the class and ask students what their favourite possession is. Try to include the words *skateboard* and *mobile phone* to prepare the students for exercise 1. Write their answers on the board and find out if there is one item more popular than the others.

Exercise 1 ⊙ 24

- Play the CD. Students listen and read, and write the correct words.
- They can compare answers in pairs.
- Check the answers with the class.
- Answer any questions about vocabulary.
- Play the CD again. Students listen and repeat chorally, then individually.

ANSWERS / AUDIO CD TRACK 24

Mark What's your favourite possession, Beth?
Beth It's my [1]mobile phone. It's cool.
Mark Is it new?
Beth Yes, it is. It's a camera phone and it's got the Internet. Have you got a [2]mobile phone?
Mark Yes, I have, but it isn't new. It's my dad's old mobile phone.
Beth What's your favourite possession, Mark?
Mark It's my [3]skateboard. It's fantastic! Have you got a [4]skateboard?
Beth No, I haven't.

You ask, You answer

- Go through the *You ask, You answer* box with the class.
- In pairs, students ask and answer the questions in the box. Encourage them to substitute the possessions with their own possessions.

Exercise 2 Pronunciation ⊙ 25

- Practise the /h/ sound with the class. Compare it to the Spanish *jota* sound and encourage students to practise the softer English sound.
- Play the CD. Students listen and repeat chorally, then individually.
- Play the CD again if necessary.

Transcript Student's Book page 24

> **Extra activity**
> - Ask students to brainstorm other words beginning with the /h/ sound. Write their answers on the board and practise their pronunciation.

Exercise 3 ⊙ 26

- Ask students to look at the photos, making sure they know how to pronounce the names and that they know what the objects are.
- Play the CD. Students listen and match the people with the objects.
- Check the answers with the class.

ANSWERS / AUDIO CD TRACK 26

1 c 2 a 3 b

1
Girl What's your favourite possession, Nathan?
Nathan It's my games console. It's fantastic.
Girl Is it new?
Nathan Yes, it is. I've got lots of new games, too. Have you got a games console?
Girl No, I haven't.

2
Boy 1 Have you got a favourite possession, Kerry?
Kerry Um ... yes, I have. It's my digital camera. It's great. Have you got a digital camera?
Boy 1 No, I haven't, but my mum's got one.

3
Boy 2 Is your games console your favourite thing, Jo?
Jo No, it isn't. My favourite possession is my laptop computer.
Boy 2 Is it new?
Jo Yes, it is. It's a birthday present. Have you got a computer?
Boy 2 Yes, I have, but it isn't new. It's my mum and dad's old computer.

> **Extra activity**
> - In pairs, students practise the dialogues in exercise 2.
> - Stronger students can substitute the objects with different objects to make their own dialogues.

Exercise 4 Pairwork

- Students tell each other about their favourite possessions, using the sample dialogue as a guide.
- Monitor and check students are swapping roles and make sure they are using *have got* correctly.
- Ask one or two students to tell the class what their partner's favourite possession is.
- Make a note of any repeated errors to check at the end of the lesson.

ANSWERS

Students' own answers.

> **Extra activity**
> Students write a description of their favourite object for homework.

Further practice
CD-ROM; Workbook page 78

Grammar page 25

have got: present simple (Interrogative and short answers)

Aim

To present *have got*: present simple interrogative and short answers

Warm-up

- Ask students a few questions using *have got*. Write a jumbled-up question with *have got* on the board for students to reorder.

Grammar box

- Go through the grammar boxes with the class and practise the pronunciation of the questions and short answers.
- Ask students to find examples of *have got* interrogative and short answers in the photo story on page 20.
- Remind students that short answers usually contain the auxiliary verb, in this case, *have*, and not the main verb.

Rules page 75

Exercise 1

- Check that the students understand the activity. They should reorder the words first to make questions and then use the picture as reference to write short answers.
- Students complete the exercise individually.
- They can compare their answers in pairs.
- Check the answers with the class.

ANSWERS
1 Have Jamie and Ellie got skateboards?
  Yes, they have.
2 Has Paul got a bike?
  Yes, he has.
3 Has Ellie got a cat?
  No, she hasn't.
4 Have Jamie and Paul got MP3 players?
  No, they haven't.
5 Has Jamie got a rucksack?
  No, he hasn't.

Exercise 2 Pairwork

- Students ask and answer questions about the things in exercise 1 using *have got*: interrogative and short answers.
- Remind them to turns to ask and answer.
- Make a note of any repeated errors to check at the end of the lesson.

ANSWERS
Students' own answers.

Extra activity
- Students continue the pairwork activity by asking each other about other possessions.
- Students can brainstorm a list of objects together before they begin the activity.

Possessive *'s*

Aims

To present the possessive *'s* and to use it when talking about possessions

Warm-up

- Books closed, go round the class and pick up a few objects that belong to different students. Say who they belong to, e.g. *This is Maria's pen. This is Enrique's ruler.*
- Ask students to guess how *Enrique's* and *Maria's* are spelt. Write the correct spellings on the board.

Grammar box

- Go through the grammar box with the class, making sure students understand how to use the possessive *'s* in English for singular and plural items. Ask why the noun *children* differs from the other nouns in the box (It's a plural noun).

Rules page 75

Exercise 3

- Students circle the correct word in the sentences.
- They can compare answers in pairs.
- Check the answers with the class.

ANSWERS
1 Katia's 2 students' 3 Lucy's 4 children's 5 dad's
6 girl's

Exercise 4 Game!

- Ask ten students to place an object on your desk. Play the game as a class.
- Monitor and check students are using the verb *be* and the possessive *'s* correctly. Make a note of any repeated errors to check at the end of the lesson.

ANSWERS
Students' own answers.

Extra activity
- Students write their own jumbled sentences using *have got* and / or the possessive *'s* for a partner to order. They can look back at *Communication* on page 24 if they need help with ideas.

Finished?

- Working individually, students write about the names of people in their family. Ask one or two students to read out their sentences to the class.

ANSWERS
Students' own answers.

Consolidation
- Remind students to make a note of the grammar rules and examples in their grammar notebook.

Further practice
CD-ROM; Workbook page 77

Skills pages 26–27

Reading

Aim

To read and understand a series of mini biographies

Background notes

- Sean Connery was born in Edinburgh in 1930. He became internationally famous in 1962 with his first James Bond film, *Dr. No*. He made seven Bond films in total. He won an academy award for his role in the 1987 film *The Untouchables* and was knighted in 2000.

- Judi Dench was born in Yorkshire in 1934 and made her professional acting debut in 1957. She went on to work in theatre, television, and film. She has won numerous awards for her work, including an academy award. She was made a Dame in 1988.

- Marge Simpson is the cartoon character wife of Homer Simpson in the hit TV show *The Simpsons*. She is famous for her blue beehive hairstyle and her role as the patient wife to Homer and mother to Bart, Lisa, and baby Maggie.

- Johnny Depp is an American actor who was born in Owensboro, Kentucky in 1963. He has starred in lots of films, including *Pirates of the Caribbean* and *Public Enemies*. His partner is the French actress and singer Vanessa Paradis with whom he has two children, Lily-Rose and Jack.

- Nick Jonas was born in 1992 and is the youngest of three brothers. As well as working together in their band, the brothers also star in a TV series called *JONAS*. Nick Jonas has also formed another band called *Nick Jonas and the Administration*, which released its first album in 2010. Nick suffers from type 1 diabetes and acts as an ambassador to help young people with the condition.

- Selena Gomez is an American actress and singer who was born in 1992 in Texas. She is best known for her role of Alex Russo in the Disney channel series *Wizards of Waverly Place*.

- ### Warm-up
- Ask students one or two questions about the people / characters in the photos, e.g. *Who are they? Do you like them? Who is your favourite?*

Exercise 1

- Ask students to read the text quickly and find the names of Nick Jonas's two brothers (Joe and Kevin).

- Students read the text silently and answer the questions. Remind them that they do not have to understand every word, but that they should look for key information to help them answer the questions.

- They can compare answers in pairs.

- Check the answers with the class.

ANSWERS

1 Sean Connery is the UK's favourite grandad.
2 She is an actor.
3 She's got blue hair.
4 Johnny Depp's children are called Lily-Rose and Jack.
6 Holly's choice for the perfect brother is Nick Jonas.
7 Selena Gomez is American.

Extra activity

- Ask students some more questions about the texts, e.g. *How many grandchildren has Sean Connery got?* (one), *Where is Judy Dench from?* (the UK), etc.

- Ask them what they think of Holly's choices for the perfect celebrity family.

Listening

Aim

To listen to a description of a family

Warm-up

- Ask a student to come to the front of the class and make true and false sentences about his or her family, e.g. *I've got seven brothers.* The other students must guess which sentences are false and correct them, e.g. *False, you've got two brothers.*

Exercise 2 💿 27

- Play the CD. Students listen and mark the sentences true or false.
- They can compare answers in pairs.
- Check the answers with the class.
- Play the CD again, pausing for students to correct the false sentences.
- They can compare answers in pairs.
- Check the answers with the class.

ANSWERS / AUDIO CD TRACK 27

1 False. He hasn't got brothers or sisters.
2 True.
3 False. His dad's a chef.
4 False. He's got three grandparents.
5 True.
6 False. He hasn't got cousins.

Hi! My name's Jack Wilson. My family is very small. Just my parents and me! I'm an only child – I haven't got brothers and sisters.
My mum's name is Helen. She's a teacher. Dad's a chef and his name's Colin. I've also got three grandparents and an aunt and uncle. My aunt's name is Claire and my uncle is Gregory. They haven't got children so I haven't got cousins.

> **Extra activity**
> - In pairs, one student makes true or false sentences about his or her family. The other student must guess which sentences are false and correct them.

Speaking

Aim

To describe your family to a partner

Exercise 3 Pairwork

- In pairs, students imagine that they are Bart or Lisa Simpson and describe their family to their partner.
- Monitor and check they are using *have got* and the possessive *'s* correctly.
- Make a note of any repeated errors to check at the end of the lesson.

ANSWERS
Students' own answers.

> **Extra activity**
> - Play *Hangman* using family words, *have got*, and the possessive *'s* in sentences.

Writing

Aim

To write a short paragraph about your family

Exercise 4

- Students read and complete the text with the missing words. Refer them back to the family tree in exercise 3. Encourage students to look at words before and after the gaps to help them work out which word is missing.
- They can compare answers in pairs.
- Check the answers with the class.

ANSWERS

1 sisters   2 Lisa   3 Maggie   4 mum's   5 name
6 got   7 grandad   8 aunts

Exercise 5

- Students write about their imaginary celebrity family.
- Tell them to look back at the reading text on page 26 for ideas, but they should choose their own celebrities.
- Monitor and check students are using the possessive *'s* and *have got* correctly.
- Remind them to make notes and prepare a rough draft.
- Students swap drafts with a partner to check and correct the mistakes.
- Students can write a final version for homework.

ANSWERS
Students' own answers.

> **Consolidation**
> - Remind students to copy any new vocabulary from the lesson into their vocabulary notebooks.

| Further practice
Workbook page 79

Grammar

be: present simple (affirmative, negative, interrogative, short answers)

Possessive *'s*

Question words

this, that, these, those

have got

Vocabulary

Adjectives

The family

Review A page 28

Vocabulary

Exercise 1

ANSWERS

1 boring 2 funny 3 terrible 4 easy

Exercise 2

ANSWERS

2 aunt 3 grandad 4 mum 5 cousin 6 sister

Grammar

Exercise 3

ANSWERS

1 I'm not English.
2 The books aren't on the desk.
3 She isn't my sister.

Exercise 4

ANSWERS

1 Is Kate Australian? No, she isn't. She's British.
2 Are they your brothers? Yes, they are.
3 Is the book interesting? No, it isn't. It's boring.

Exercise 5

ANSWERS

1 dad's 2 've got 3 's got 4 haven't got 5 've got
6 friend's 7 've got 8 Have you got

Exercise 6

ANSWERS

1 Who 2 isn't 3 is he 4 This 5 Where 6 she is
7 those 8 have

My Progress

• Students read the sentences and choose the faces that are true for them.

• If students have fewer than three smiley faces, encourage them to review the grammar or vocabulary of the previous two units and do more practice.

Songs

• The following songs would be appropriate to use at this point:

• *True Colors* by Glee Cast (adjectives)

• *I've got you* by McFly (subject pronouns and *be*)

• *How deep is your love* by Take That (subject / object pronouns, possessive adjectives)

• *Listen, do you want to know a secret?* by The Beatles (subject pronouns, possessive adjectives)

• *Hearts collide* by Green Day (*be*)

Culture club

Grammar

be: present simple (affirmative, negative, interrogative, short answers)

Question words

Possessive *'s*

Vocabulary

Countries and nationalities

Adjectives

Topic

Multiculturalism

Geography: English-speaking countries

Culture club A page 29

Aim

To read and understand a text about English-speaking countries

Warm-up

- Ask students to look at the photo, the flags, and the introduction, and ask questions, e.g. *What are the names of the countries?* (the UK, Canada, the US, Australia) *Who can you see?* (Four boys) *Who are they?* (They are a pop band).

Background notes

- London is the capital city of the UK and is in the south of England. It has a population of about 7,600,000. Some famous landmarks in London are Buckingham Palace, Big Ben, the London Eye, and Tower Bridge.
- Washington DC is the capital of the US. It is on the north bank of the Potomac River and has borders with the states of Virginia and Maryland. It has a population of about 600,000. The White House, home of the US president, is in Washington DC, as well as other famous tourist attractions such as the Thomas Jefferson Memorial.
- Elk Point is in the Canadian province of Alberta in the central east area and has a population of about 1,400.
- Ottawa is the capital of Canada and is in the province of Ontario. It is on the southern banks of the Ottawa River and it has a population of about 812,000.
- Canberra is the capital city of Australia and has a population of more than 345,000. It is in the south east of the country.
- Darwin is on the north coast of Australia in the Northern Territory. It has a population of about 120,600 and is the largest city in that part of Australia.

Exercise 1

- Draw students' attention to the *Look!* box and remind them that the UK is made up of four different countries. If you have a world map, put it on the board and ask students to point to the different countries in the UK.
- Students read the text in detail and answer the questions. They can work with a partner.
- Check the answers with the class, asking students to give you the full answer.

ANSWERS
1 Their name is *One World*.
2 He's sixteen years old.
3 His favourite city is Ottawa.
4 He's from Darwin, in Australia.
5 Robbie, Dylan, and Jason aren't from a capital city.

Extra activity: Capital city quiz

- Call out the names of countries for students, in small groups, to give you the capital city.
- If you have a world map, point to a country on it and ask groups to give you the capital city.
- The group with the most correct answers is the winner.

Exercise 2 Focus on you

- Students read the questions and make notes to answer them. Encourage them to give as much detail as possible.
- In pairs, students ask and answer about where their partner is from.
- Ask one or two pairs to report back to the class.
- If there are students from countries other than the one you are in, ask them to talk a little more about their country.

ANSWERS
Students' own answers.

Extra activity

- Give students a few minutes to read the text again and to remember as much as they can.
- Books closed. Ask questions and see how much students can remember, e.g. *Where is Robbie from? Which country is Elk Point in? What colour is the Canadian flag? How old is Danny?*, etc.

Further practice

Workbook pages 70–79

③ We get up at seven

Grammar
Present simple (affirmative; spelling variations – 3rd person singular)

Adverbs of frequency

Prepositions of time

Vocabulary
Daily routines

Communication
Talking about TV programmes

/s/ /z/ /ɪz/

Falling intonation in *Wh-* questions

Skills
Reading: A Musical Sensation

Listening: Daily routine

Speaking: Describe your daily routine

Writing: Your favourite day of the week

Topics
Multiculturalism: Daily life and routines

Presentation page 30

Aim
To present the new language in a motivating context

Story
Two actors, Claire and Jason, have come to talk to the students at Star Academy about their work and daily routine. Holly decides she would like to play the part of Suzannah in the musical, but Ruby thinks she is the perfect person to play Suzannah, not Holly.

Warm-up
• Ask students what they can remember from the last part of the photo story.

• Ask them to look at the photo and ask questions, e.g. *Who are the people in the photo?* (Mr Lane, Alex, Holly, Jazz, Ruby, Luke, and another student) *Where are they?* (In the school theatre/hall).

Exercise 1 Read and listen 28
• Explain that students must read and listen, and decide who Jason and Claire are.

• Play the CD. Students read and listen.

ANSWER

c actors

• Go through the *Check it out!* box and make sure students understand the phrases.

• Check any other unknown vocabulary in the text.

• Students listen again and repeat chorally, then individually.

Transcript   Student's Book page 30

Exercise 2 Comprehension
• Students match the sentence halves individually.

• They can compare answers in pairs.

• Check the answers with the class.

ANSWERS

1 b   2 c   3 a

Extra activity
• In small groups, students act out the dialogue in exercise 1.

Consolidation
• Remind students to copy any new words or phrases into their vocabulary notebooks.

Language focus page 31

Aim
To practise the target language in a new context

Exercise 3 Dialogue focus
• Students read the dialogues individually, and find and correct the mistakes.

• Encourage students to look at the photos to help them find the answers and remind them they can look back at exercise 1.

• They can compare answers in pairs. Do not check answers at this point.

Exercise 4 29
• Play the CD. Students listen and check their answers to exercise 3.

• Students listen again and repeat chorally, then individually.

ANSWERS / AUDIO CD TRACK 29

1

Alex Jason, what's your typical day like?

Jason I usually get up at half past **eleven** in the morning.

2

Jason Then, I sometimes have breakfast, and I **always** go to the gym.

Claire He always has breakfast and he **never** goes to the gym!

3

Holly Have you got a big part in the **musical**?

Claire Yes, I have. I'm Suzannah. She**'s** an important character.

Exercise 5 Focus on you

- Students complete the sentences individually.
- Remind them to look back at the dialogue in exercise 1 if necessary.
- Check the answers with the class.

ANSWERS

1 get   **2** have   **3** go

Exercise 6 Pairwork

- In pairs, students tell their partner if the sentences they completed in exercise 5 are true or false for them.
- Monitor and check that students swap roles.

ANSWERS

Students' own answers.

Vocabulary   page 32

Daily routines

Aim

To present and practise the language for daily routines: *do my homework, get home, get up, go to bed, go to school, have a shower, have breakfast, have dinner, have lunch*

Warm-up

- Ask students what time they get up in the morning, on a weekday and at the weekend.
- Do a quick review of days of the week and times if necessary at this point.

Exercise 1   ⊚ 30

- Students match the sentences (a–i) with the pictures (1–9).
- Draw students' attention to the *Look!* box, making sure they know that these expressions take *have* in English.
- Play the CD. Students listen and check their answers.
- Students listen again and repeat chorally, then individually.

ANSWERS / AUDIO CD TRACK 30

1 d I get up at seven o'clock.
2 b I have a shower at ten past seven.
3 i I have breakfast at half past seven.
4 e I go to school at twenty past eight.
5 a I have lunch at one o'clock.
6 g I go home at four o'clock.
7 f I have dinner at six o'clock.
8 c I do my homework at quarter past seven.
9 h I go to bed at ten o'clock.

Extra activity 1

- Give students a few minutes to look at the pictures.
- Books closed. Call out the number of a picture for students to give you the expression, e.g. T: *4* SS: *go to school.*

Extra activity 2

- Give students a few minutes to memorize the daily routine expressions.
- Call out the words without the verbs for students to give you the appropriate verb, e.g. T: *lunch* SS: *have*, etc.

Exercise 2 Pairwork

- Students make a note of when they do the activities in exercise 1.
- In pairs, students exchange information about their daily routines.
- Monitor and check that students swap roles and make a note of any repeated errors to check at the end of the lesson.
- See if there are any interesting routines to report to the class.

ANSWERS

Students' own answers.

Extra activity 1

- Draw some clock faces on the board and ask for volunteers to come out and put a time on the clock face. The others guess which daily routine is done at that time.

Extra activity 2

- In small groups, students mime one of the daily routines for others to guess which routine it is.

Consolidation

- Remind students to copy the daily routine phrases into their vocabulary books and to make a note of the phrases in a way that will help them remember them.

Further practice
CD-ROM; Workbook page 81

Grammar page 33

Present simple (Affirmative)

Aim

To present and practise the present simple affirmative form

Warm-up

- Say *I get up at seven o'clock.* Then point to a student and say *(Luis) gets up at ...* Ask the student to complete the sentence with the time. Write the two sentences on the board. Elicit their meanings and the tense (present simple). Ask students why the verb in the second sentence has an *s* (It's the third person singular form).

Grammar box

- Go through the grammar box with the class.
- Draw students' attention to the third person singular *-s.* Highlight the difference between this and the other persons.
- You can write the verb on the board and then draw the third person *-s* in a different colour to help students remember it. Give students another example for them to give you the third person singular form, e.g. T: *listen* SS: *listens*.
- Ask students to find more examples in the dialogue on page 30.

Rules page 80

Exercise 1

- Students complete the exercise individually. Remind them to check what the subject of the verb is before they decide which verb is correct.
- They can compare answers in pairs.
- Check the answers with the class.

ANSWERS
1 gets 2 sleep 3 writes 4 listen 5 speaks 6 live

Present simple (Spelling variations – 3rd person singular)

Aim

To present and practise the present simple spelling variations in the third person singular

Grammar box

- Go through the grammar box with the class, making sure students are aware of the third person spelling changes.
- Give students a few minutes to study the verbs in the box.
- Books closed. Call out a verb from the box and ask for volunteers to spell the third person singular form.
- Refer students to the rules.

Rules page 80

Exercise 2

- Students complete the sentences with the present simple form individually.
- Remind them to think carefully about the spelling of each verb and to look back at the grammar box if necessary.
- Check the answers with the class.

ANSWERS
1 finishes 2 has 3 watches 4 cries 5 studies
6 goes

Extra activity

- Books closed. Write a list of verbs in the infinitive on the board and ask students to come to the board and write the third person singular form. This could be done in teams. The team with the most correct answers wins.

Exercise 3 Pronunciation 31

- Go through the pronunciation box and model the pronunciation of the different endings.
- Play the CD. Students listen and repeat chorally, then individually.

Transcript Student's Book page 33

Exercise 4 32

- Before you begin the exercise, write the target verbs on the board in their infinitive form (look, wash, read, get, play, teach).
- Play the CD. Students listen and write the verbs in the correct column. They can look at the infinitive forms of the verbs on the board for help with spelling.
- Check the answers with the class. You can copy the table onto the board and ask students to fill in the answers.
- Students listen again and repeat chorally, then individually.

ANSWERS / AUDIO CD TRACK 32
looks washes reads gets plays teaches
/s/ **looks, gets**   /z/ **reads, plays**   /ɪz/ **washes, teaches**

Extra activity 1

- If students need more practice, call out third person singular verbs for students to give the correct pronunciation for the ending, e.g. T: *speaks* SS: *s.*

Extra activity 2

- Play *Hangman* to practise the spelling variations of the 3rd person singular form.

Exercise 5

- Students complete the text with the correct form of the verbs in the box.
- Remind them to look back at the grammar boxes if necessary.
- Check the answers with the class.

ANSWERS
1 gets up 2 have 3 watches 4 go 5 goes 6 get
7 do 8 listens 9 read 10 plays 11 go 12 goes

Finished?

- Students look at the pictures on page 32 and write about the girl's routine, using the third person singular.
- Remind them to check the third person verb forms.
- Students can compare sentences in pairs.
- Ask a few students to read their sentences out to the class. Make sure that in sentence 9 (or sentence c) they change 'my' to 'her'.

1 She gets up at seven o'clock.
2 She has a shower at ten past seven.
3 She has breakfast at half past seven.
4 She goes to school at twenty past eight.
5 She has lunch at one o'clock.
6 She gets home at four o'clock.
7 She has dinner at six o'clock.
8 She does her homework at quarter past seven.
9 She goes to bed at ten o'clock.

Extra activity

- Call out the infinitive form of a verb for students to give you the third person singular, e.g. T: *have*   SS: *has*.

Consolidation

- Remind students to make a note of the grammar and the rules in their grammar notebooks.

Further practice
CD-ROM; Workbook pages 81–82

Communication page 34

Talking about TV programmes

Aim

To ask and answer questions about your favourite TV programmes

Background notes

- *The Simpsons* is an American animated TV sitcom. It was created by Matt Groening and was first broadcast in 1989. The Simpsons live in Springfield and they are Homer (Dad), Marge (Mum), Lisa, Bart, and Maggie (the children). It is the longest-running American sitcom.
- The *Wizards of Waverly Place* is a Disney channel series which was first shown in 2007. Selena Gomez stars in the series, which is about the three Russo siblings who have magical powers. The show is set in Waverly Sub Station, a sandwich shop run by the children's parents and where they sometimes help out.

Warm-up

- Ask students what programmes they like to watch on TV and give one or two examples if necessary, e.g. *The Simpsons*.

Exercise 1 34

- Ask students to read the factfile before they complete the dialogue with the missing information.
- They can compare answers in pairs.
- Play the CD. Students listen and check their answers.
- Students listen again and repeat chorally, then individually.

Jane What's your favourite TV programme, David?
David My favourite TV programme is **1**The Simpsons. It's fantastic!
Jane What day is it on?
David It's on **2**Tuesdays and **3**Fridays.
Jane What time is it on?
David It's on at **4**6 o'clock.
Jane What channel is it on?
David It's on **5**Channel 4.

You ask, You answer

- Go through the *You ask, You answer* box as a class.
- In pairs, students ask and answer using the examples in the box.
- Monitor and check that students are using the correct intonation and review as necessary.

Exercise 2 Pronunciation 34

- Read aloud the questions in the *You ask, You answer* box to show students how the intonation falls in information questions.
- Play the CD. Students read and listen.
- Students listen again and repeat chorally, then individually.

Transcript   Student's Book page 34

Extra activity

- If students need more practice, say the questions from the *You ask, You answer* box starting from the end for students to repeat chorally, then individually, e.g. *on?, it on?, is it on?, day is it on?, What day is it on?*, etc.

Exercise 3 Pairwork

- Students complete the dialogue with information about themselves.
- In pairs, students ask and answer to find out about their partner.
- Students report back to the class on their partner's favourite TV programme.

Students' own answers.

Extra activity

- Students can vote and see if the class has a favourite TV programme.

Further practice
CD-ROM; Workbook page 83

Grammar page 35

Adverbs of frequency

Aim

To present and practise adverbs of frequency

Warm-up

- Say *I get up at seven o'clock on Monday, Tuesday, Wednesday, Thursday, Friday, Saturday, and Sunday*. Write the sentence on the board. Then say *I always get up at seven o'clock*, and write it on the board. Circle the word *always* and elicit its meaning. Explain that it is an adverb of frequency: it describes how often we do things. Ask students if they know any other adverbs of frequency.

Grammar box

- Go through the grammar box with the class, explaining the different points between *always* and *never* on the timeline.
- Give students an example of something you always do and something you never do, and elicit one or two examples from the class using the other adverbs of frequency.
- Ask students to look back at the dialogue on page 30 and to find more examples of adverbs of frequency.
- Monitor and check that students are using the present simple correctly.
- Students read the sentences and choose the correct words in rules 1 and 2.

Rules page 80

ANSWERS
1 after   2 before

Exercise 1

- Individually, students order the words to write sentences.
- Monitor and check they are putting the adverb of frequency in the correct place and refer them to the grammar box if necessary.
- Check the answers with the class.

ANSWERS
1 He usually gets up at eight o'clock.
2 Our English lessons are always interesting.
3 We often play football in the park.
4 She never reads her emails.

Exercise 2

- Students look at the picture and write sentences about Danny, using the cues.
- They can compare answers in pairs.
- Check the answers with the class.

ANSWERS
1 He sometimes goes to the cinema.   2 He is usually happy.   3 He always has lunch at school.   4 He never reads books.   5 He rarely tidies his room.

> ### Extra activity
> - In pairs, students write jumbled-up sentences with adverbs of frequency for their partner to reorder.

Prepositions of time

Aim

To present and practise prepositions of time

Warm-up

- Say *I have breakfast at ten o'clock on Sundays*, and write the sentence on the board. Circle the words *at* and *on*, and elicit their meanings. Explain that they are prepositions of time. Point out that students should not try to translate prepositions of time from their L1 directly into English.

Grammar box

- Go through the grammar box with the class. Make sure students understand when to use each preposition of time.

Rules page 80

Exercise 3

- Students choose the correct word in each sentence.
- They can compare answers in pairs.
- Check the answers with the class.

ANSWERS
1 in   2 at   3 on   4 in   5 at   6 on

> ### Extra activity
> - Call out some time expressions for students to give you the correct preposition of time, e.g. T: *Saturdays* SS: *on*, etc.

Exercise 4 Game!

- In pairs, students make sentences about themselves and their best friend using the verbs.
- Monitor and check that students are using the first and third person present simple correctly and encourage them to use adverbs of frequency.
- Make sure students swap roles.
- Ask one or two pairs to tell the rest of the class about their best friend.

ANSWERS
Students' own answers.

Finished?

- Students write six true sentences about their daily routine using the present simple and adverbs of frequency.
- Encourage students to swap sentences and to tell each other about their routines.
- Ask one or two pairs to tell the rest of the class about their partner's routine, using the third person singular.

ANSWERS
Students' own answers.

> ### Extra activity
> - Students think of their favourite film star, sportsperson, etc. and write sentences about their daily routine.

> ### Consolidation
> - Remind students to make a note of the grammar rules and examples in their grammar notebooks.

Further practice
CD-ROM; Workbook page 82

Skills pages 36–37

Reading

Aims

To read and understand a magazine text; to complete a summary about it

Warm-up

- Ask students to look at the magazine article and see if they know the musical. Ask *What is a musical?* and *Do you know the story of Billy Elliot?*

Background notes

- *Billy Elliot* is a British film which was released in 2000. It tells the story of a young boy growing up in a fictional northern town who wants to be a dancer, but whose father struggles to accept this. The film is set during the UK miners' strike of 1984–85. The film went on to be a big hit in theatres in the UK from 2005 and it was taken to Broadway in 2008. The musical has won many awards.

Exercise 1

- Explain to students that the text is in two parts: one about an actor, Callum Kennedy, the other about the musical, *Billy Elliot*.
- Ask students to scan the text about Callum and to find out how many brothers he has (three).
- Students then read the text carefully. Remind them they do not have to understand every word.
- Individually, students complete the summary. Remind them to think about words before and after the gaps to help them with the context.
- Check any unknown vocabulary with the class.
- Students can compare answers with a partner or you can do this as a whole-class activity.

ANSWERS

1 brothers   2 London   3 actors   4 Billy
5 ballet dancer   6 very happy   7 lessons
8 famous ballet dancer

Extra activity 1

- Use the summary text as a dictation activity. Read out each sentence for students to listen and copy.

Extra activity 2

- Ask students what they think about working in the theatre. Would they take a role like Billy?

Listening

Aim

To listen to and understand an actor talking about his daily routine

Exercise 2 ⊚ 35

- Encourage students to read the answer options before they listen to the CD.
- Play the CD. Students listen and choose the correct answer.
- They can compare answers in pairs.
- Play the CD again. Students listen and check their answers.

ANSWERS / AUDIO CD TRACK 35

1 b   2 a   3 b   4 b   5 a

Hi! I'm Matt. I live with Callum and Sarah with our host family in London – we all work in the theatre.
We don't get up very early. We get up at eight o'clock and we have a shower. Then we have breakfast. We don't go to school because we have private lessons. Our teachers come to our house and we have lessons for three hours every day. After lunch we go to the theatre. We practise songs and dance routines for two or three hours, then we relax and have dinner at six o'clock. The show starts at eight o'clock and finishes at ten o'clock. After the show we go back to the house. We usually go to bed at 11 o'clock. We're always very tired!

Speaking

Aim

To describe your own daily routine

Exercise 3 Pairwork

- Students use the information in the box to write sentences about their own daily routine.
- In pairs, students describe their daily routine to their partner.
- Monitor and check students are using the present simple correctly and that they are putting adverbs of frequency in the correct place. Make a note of any repeated errors to check at the end of the lesson.
- Ask one or two pairs to report back to the class on their partner's routine.

ANSWERS

Students' own answers.

Extra activity 1

- Write *play computer games* on the board.
- Give students two minutes to see how many words they can make from the three words.

Extra activity 2

- Write anagrams of daily routines expressions on the board for students to solve.
- This can be done as a whole class or with students separated into groups. The first group to solve all the anagrams wins.

Writing

Aim

To write a short paragraph about your favourite day of the week

Exercise 4

• Students read the notes and the message.

• Individually, students complete the message, using the information in the notes.

• Remind them to look before and after each gap to help them work out which word is missing.

• Students can compare answers in pairs.

• Check the answers with the class.

ANSWERS

1 have breakfast   2 watch TV   3 meet my friends
4 drama lessons   5 to the cinema   6 listen to
7 read emails   8 write to my e-friends

> **Extra activity 1**
>
> • Ask students if they do similar things to Josie at the weekend.

> **Extra activity 2**
>
> • Ask students to mime activities they do at weekends for the rest of the class to guess.

Exercise 5

• Students use the text in exercise 4 as a model to write about their own favourite day.

• Encourage them to make notes first and to write a draft version.

• Students swap draft versions with a partner to correct.

• They can write their final version in class or for homework.

ANSWERS

Students' own answers.

> **Consolidation**
>
> • Remind students to copy any new vocabulary into their vocabulary notebooks.

Further practice
Workbook page 84

4 Do you like your new school?

Grammar
Present simple (negative, interrogative and short answers)

Question words + present simple

How often ...?

Object pronouns

Vocabulary
Sports

Communication
Talking about likes and dislikes

Rising intonation in *yes / no* questions and falling intonation in *Wh-* questions

Skills
Reading: Hannah swims to success

Listening: Mark talking about his school

Speaking: Ask and answer questions about sports

Writing: Your favourite school day and sports

Topics
Health: Fitness through sport

Presentation page 38

Aim
To present the new language in a motivating context

Story
Holly is talking to her dad about Star Academy. During her conversation, she receives an unexpected call from Ruby.

Warm-up
- Review the last part of the photo story.
- Ask students to look at the photo. Ask questions, e.g. *Who is in the photo?* (Holly and her dad) *Where are they?* (In Holly's house) *Which room are they in?* (In the living room) *What is there in the room?* (a table, a chair, books, fruit, a sofa, a picture, shoes, plants, a TV).

Exercise 1 Read and listen 36
- Play the CD. Students read and listen to answer the question.
- Go through the *Check it out!* box and make sure students understand the expressions.
- Check any other unknown vocabulary in the text.
- Students listen again and repeat chorally, then individually.

ANSWER

c They are talking about the teachers and students.

Transcript   Student's Book page 38

Exercise 2 Comprehension
- Students read the sentences and choose the correct answer, referring back to the dialogue as necessary.
- They can compare answers in pairs.
- Check the answers with the class, encouraging students to read out the complete sentences.

ANSWERS

1 every morning   2 after school   3 likes   4 phones

Extra activity
- In pairs, students act out the dialogue.

Consolidation
- Remind students to copy any new words or phrases into their vocabulary notebooks.

Language focus page 39

Aim
To practise the target language in a new context

Exercise 3 Dialogue focus
- Students read the dialogues and write the questions.
- They can compare answers in pairs. Do not check the answers at this point.

Exercise 4 37
- Play the CD. Students listen and check their answers to exercise 3.
- Students listen again and repeat chorally, then individually.

ANSWERS / AUDIO CD TRACK 37

a

Dad Do you like your new school, Holly?

Holly Yes, I do. I love it.

Dad ¹How often do you have maths and English?

Holly Oh, we don't study boring subjects!

Dad What?

b

Dad ²And, do you like the students?

Holly Yes, I really like them. But not Ruby. I don't like her at all!

c

Holly ³Who is it?

Dad It's Ruby.

Holly Ruby??!

Exercise 5 Focus on you
- Students put the words in the correct order.
- Remind them to think about word order in questions and to look back at the dialogue in exercise 3 if necessary.
- Students can compare answers in pairs.
- Monitor and help as necessary. Make a note of any repeated errors to check at the end of the lesson.

B Yes, I do.

A How often do you have maths and English?

B We have them every morning.

Exercise 6 Pairwork

- In pairs, students practise the dialogue in exercise 5.
- Monitor for pronunciation and make sure they swap roles.

Extra activity

- In pairs, students can act out the dialogue in exercise 5 for the class.

Vocabulary page 40

Sports

Aim

To present and practise sports vocabulary and collocations with *play* (*basketball*, *football*, *tennis*), *go* (*cycling*, *skiing*, *swimming*), and *do* (*athletics*, *gymnastics*, *karate*)

Warm-up

- Ask students if they do any sports. If so, which ones? If not, ask them if they like watching sports live or on TV.

Exercise 1 38

- Individually, students match the pictures of sports with the words in the box.
- Tell them to look at the verb which goes with each sport below the picture and to try and learn the two words together.
- Play the CD. Students listen and check their answers.
- Students listen again and repeat chorally, then individually.

ANSWERS / AUDIO CD TRACK 38

play football   **1** do gymnastics   **2** go swimming
3 do athletics   **4** go cycling   **5** play basketball
6 play tennis   **7** go skiing   **8** do karate

Extra activity

- Give students a few minutes to look at and remember the pictures.
- Books closed. Call out the number of a picture for students to say the sport, e.g. T: *1* SS: *do gymnastics*.

Exercise 2

- Students write the names of the sports in exercise 1 under the correct heading.
- Remind them to look back at exercise 1 again if necessary, but encourage stronger students to cover exercise 1.
- Check the answers with the class.

ANSWERS

1 basketball   **2** tennis   **3** swimming   **4** cycling
5 skiing   **6** gymnastics   **7** athletics   **8** karate

Extra activity

- Give students a few minutes to look at the pictures in exercise 1.
- Books closed. Call out a sport and ask students to say *play*, *go*, or *do*, e.g. T: *skiing* SS: *go*.

Exercise 3 Pairwork

- In pairs, students talk about sports they play and don't play.
- Remind them to use the present simple and adverbs of frequency. They can refer to the example if necessary.
- Ask students to tell the rest of the class about what their partner plays / doesn't play.
- Ask one or two pairs to tell the rest of the class about their partner.

ANSWERS

Students' own answers.

Extra activity 1

- Students choose a sport from exercise 1 and mime it for the rest of the class to guess.

Extra activity 2

- In small groups or as a whole class, students play *Hangman* with the sports from this lesson.

Extra activity 3

- Write anagrams of the sports from exercise 1 on the board for the class to solve.

Consolidation

- Encourage students to copy the vocabulary from this lesson into their vocabulary notebooks. Remind them to record the vocabulary in a way that will be helpful for them to remember it.

Further practice

CD-ROM; Workbook page 86

Grammar page 41

Present simple (Negative)

Aim

To present and practise the present simple negative

Warm-up

- Ask a student a question that is certain to get the answer *no*, for example: *Do you have ice cream for breakfast?* Write the question on the board. Then write *I don't have ice cream for breakfast.* Circle *don't* and elicit that it makes verbs negative in the present simple.
- Keep the question and sentence on the board.

Grammar box

- Go through the grammar box with the class. Draw students' attention to the full and short negative forms.
- Practise the pronunciation of the different forms.
- Remind students of how the third person singular affirmative form is different from the others and tell them that this is the same in the negative form.
- Ask students to look back at the dialogue on page 32 and to find more examples of the present simple negative.

Rules page 85

Exercise 1

- Individually, students complete the sentences with *don't* or *doesn't*. They can refer to the grammar box if necessary.
- Check the answers with the class.

> **ANSWERS**
> 1 doesn't 2 don't 3 don't 4 doesn't
> 5 doesn't 6 don't

Exercise 2

- Individually, students correct the sentences using the words in brackets.
- Remind them to use the third person -*s* and *don't* / *doesn't* carefully.
- Check the answers with the class.

> **ANSWERS**
> 1 He doesn't go swimming on Saturday. He goes swimming on Sunday.
> 2 They don't get home at half past three. They get home at half past four.
> 3 You don't do karate with my cousin. You do karate with my brother.
> 4 My dad doesn't speak French. My dad speaks German.
> 5 My mum doesn't work in a sports centre. My mum works in a school.

> **Extra activity**
> - In pairs, students tell each other how they do things differently in the holidays, using the sentences in exercise 1 as an example, e.g. *I don't get up at seven o'clock. I get up at eleven o'clock.* Ask some students to report back to the class about their partner.

Interrogative and short answers

Aim

To present and practise the present simple interrogative and short answers

Warm-up

- Go back to the question and sentence written on the board at the beginning of the grammar activities. Circle *Do* in the question and explain that it is used in the present simple question form.
- Ask the students a few questions using *do*. They can answer *yes* or *no* at this point.

Grammar box

- Go through the grammar boxes with the class. Point out the use of the auxiliary in questions and the fact that we do not repeat the main verb in short answers.
- Practise the pronunciation of the questions and short answers with the class.

Rules page 85

Exercise 3

- Students complete the questions and short answers.
- They can compare answers in pairs.
- Check the answers with the class.

> **ANSWERS**
> 1 Do; don't 2 Do; do 3 Does; does 4 Does; doesn't
> 5 Do; don't 6 Do; do

Exercise 4

- Students write questions and short answers using the prompts and illustrations.
- They can compare answers in pairs.
- Check the answers with the class.

> **ANSWERS**
> 1 Do you like football? No, I don't.
> 2 Does Pablo study maths? Yes, he does.
> 3 Does your mum get up at six o'clock? No, she doesn't.
> 4 Does Anna go cycling? Yes, she does.

Finished?

- Using the sample question and answer as a guide, students work in pairs to write a dialogue between themselves. They should write five questions and answers.
- Check that students are using *do* and *don't* correctly.

> **ANSWERS**
> Students' own answers.

> **Extra activity**
> - In pairs, students write jumbled-up questions in the present simple for their partners to reorder.

> **Consolidation**
> - Remind students to copy the grammar rules into their grammar notebooks. Encourage them to record the rules in a way that is helpful for them to remember.

Further practice
CD-ROM; Workbook pages 86–87

Communication page 42

Talking about likes and dislikes

Aim

To ask and answer about things you like / don't like

Warm-up

• Ask one or two questions, e.g. *Do you like sports? Do you like football? Do you like The Simpsons?* and elicit answers.

Background notes

• Avril Lavigne is a Canadian singer-songwriter. She was born in Belleville, Ontario in 1984. She has sold more than 30 million copies of her albums worldwide. Her best known hits are *Complicated* and *Sk8er Boi*.

Exercise 1 ⊚ 39

• Ask students to look at the photos and the information table. Explain the emoticon symbols in the table if necessary.

• Practise the pronunciation of *science* /ˈsaɪəns/ and *spiders* /ˈspaɪdəz/.

• Students complete the dialogue individually using information from the table.

• They can compare answers in pairs.

• Play the CD. Students listen and check their answers.

ANSWERS / AUDIO CD TRACK 39

Max Do you like Avril Lavigne?
Sarah Yes, I do. I love her. What about you?
Max I really like her, but I prefer ¹Lady Gaga.
Sarah What do you think of ²science?
Max I quite like it. And you?
Sarah I don't like it very much.
Max And, do you like ³spiders?
Sarah No, I don't! I don't like them at all! What about you?
Max I hate them!

You ask, You answer

• Read through the *You ask, You answer* box with the class.

• In pairs, students can ask and answer the questions in the box.

Exercise 2 Pronunciation ⊚ 40

• Go through the pronunciation box with the class, reminding students of how intonation falls in *Wh*-questions. Model the pronunciation of the *Yes / No* questions so students can hear how the pronunciation rises.

• Play the CD. Students listen.

• Students listen again and repeat chorally, then individually.

Transcript Student's Book page 42

Extra activity 1

• If students need more practice, read each question out starting from the end for students to repeat chorally, then individually, e.g. *sport?, like sport?, you like sport?, Do you like sport?*

Extra activity 2

• In pairs, students ask and answer the questions in the pronunciation box, giving true answers about themselves.

• Monitor and check for appropriate use of short answers in *Yes / No* questions and appropriate responses to *Wh*-questions.

• Pairs can report back to the class.

Exercise 3 Pairwork

• In pairs, students ask and answer about the people and things in the box.

• Remind them to look back at the *You ask, You answer* box for different ways to reply.

• Monitor and check students are asking and answering correctly and make a note of any repeated errors to check at the end of the lesson.

• Ask one or two pairs to report back their views to the class.

ANSWERS
Students' own answers.

Extra activity

• Students look back at the *You answer* box in exercise 2 and classify the replies from positive to negative.

▌Further practice
CD-ROM; Workbook page 88

Grammar page 43

Question words

Aim

To present and practise question words in present simple questions

Warm-up

- Write gapped versions of question words on the board for students to complete and check their meanings.

Grammar box

- Go through the grammar box with the class. Point out the use of the auxiliary in questions and elicit the difference between the singular and plural auxiliary form.
- Explain that *do* and *does* in *Wh-* questions have a weak pronunciation: /də/ and /dəz/.

Rules page 85

Exercise 1

- Students read the information about Holly's day in the brackets and write questions and answers using the prompts.
- Monitor and check for correct use of questions and the present simple in the answers.
- Students can compare answers in pairs.
- Check the answers with the class.

ANSWERS
1 What time does she start school?
   She starts school at 9.00 a.m.
2 Where does she have lunch?
   She has lunch at school.
3 When does she finish school?
   She finishes school at 3.30 p.m.
4 What does she do after school?
   She does (her) homework after school.

> **Extra activity**
> - In pairs, students ask and answer the questions about Holly's day. Remind them to swap roles.
> - Check that they are using the correct subject pronouns and *do* or *does* appropriately.

How often …?

Aim

To present and practise *How often …?* and expressions of frequency

Warm-up

- Write the following on the board: *How often do you go shopping? I go shopping three times a week.*
- Circle *How often* and *three times a week* and elicit their meanings.

Grammar box

- Go through the grammar box with the class. Draw students' attention to the different ways of expressing frequency.

Exercise 2

- Individually, students write *How often* questions and then answer them for themselves.
- Check the answers with the class, encouraging students to give you their own answers.

ANSWERS
1 How often do you study Japanese at school?
2 How often do you have pizza for dinner?
3 How often do you play sports?
Students' own answers.

Rules page 85

> **Extra activity**
> - In pairs, students ask and answer the questions in exercise 2.
> - Ask pairs to report back to the class on how often their partner does things.

Object pronouns

Aim

To present and practise object pronouns

Warm-up

- Write *I like it.* on the board and ask which are the subject and object pronouns. Explain that subject pronouns always precede the verb and object pronouns always follow it.

Grammar box

- Go through the grammar box with the class.
- Write sample sentences on the board so that students can see where subject and object pronouns are placed in sentences.

Rules page 85

Exercise 3

- Individually, students complete the sentences with the correct object pronouns.
- Check the answers with the class, asking students to read out the complete sentence.

ANSWERS
1 them   2 her   3 him   4 it   5 us   6 me

> **Extra activity**
> - On the board write a column of subject pronouns and a column of object pronouns beside it, but in a different order.
> - Ask students to come to the board and draw lines to match the subject and object pronouns.

Exercise 4 Game!

- In pairs, students ask and answer questions using the verbs in the football.
- The student with the most correct questions is the winner.

ANSWERS
Students' own answers.

Finished?

- Students write five questions to ask their favourite sports star.

ANSWERS

Students' own answers.

> ### Consolidation
> - Encourage students to make a note of the grammar and the rules in their grammar notebooks, and to learn the rules.

Further practice
CD-ROM; Workbook page 87

Skills pages 44–45

Reading

Aim

To read a magazine article about the daily routine of a young British swimmer

Warm-up

- Ask students *What is the sport in the photos?* (swimming) *Is the girl good at swimming?* (Yes).
- Ask a couple more questions to help students predict what is in the text, e.g. *When does she practise?* (Possible answers: before and after school. At weekends.) *Has she got a lot of free time?* (Possible answer: No, she hasn't.) Write students' predictions on the board to review at the end of the activity.

Exercise 1

- Individually, students read the text and decide what it is about.
- Check the answer with the class.

ANSWER

b A young British sports star

Exercise 2

- Students read the text again and answer the questions.
- Encourage them to think about the kind of information they will be looking for in each answer.
- Help with any new vocabulary as necessary.
- Check the answers with the class, encouraging students to give you the full answer.

ANSWERS

1 She's fourteen.
2 She wants to represent Britain in the Olympics and win a gold medal.
3 She gets up at five o'clock in the morning.
4 She goes swimming for two hours before school.
5 She doesn't meet her friends very often.

> ### Extra activity
> - In pairs, students discuss the differences between their daily routine and Hannah's.
> - Ask pairs to report back to the class. Does anyone have a routine like Hannah's?

Listening

Aim

To listen to and understand a teenager talking about school

Warm-up

- Ask students to look at the photo. Ask how old they think Mark is, and what his favourite school subject is. Write their ideas on the board, or ask students to write them, to revise the spelling of school subjects.
- Ask a few students what their favourite school day is, and why. Pre-teach *double lesson*, and ask students when they have double lessons, and if they enjoy them.

Exercise 3 41

- Encourage students to read the answer options before they listen.
- Play the CD. Students listen and answer the questions.
- Check the answers with the class and play the CD again if necessary.

ANSWERS / AUDIO CD TRACK 41

1 b   2 b   3 a   4 a   5 c

Alice What's your favourite school day, Mark?
Mark Um... It's Monday, actually.
Alice Monday?! Are you serious? I hate Monday!
Mark Yes, really! It isn't a joke! I like Monday. We have double art on Monday afternoon and that's my favourite subject. And then, after school, I go to Photography Club and I love it. I'm quite good at photography. I've got a digital camera and I use it a lot.
Alice My favourite day is Wednesday because we have double P.E. and I usually play volleyball. I love it!
Mark Ugh! P.E.! I hate sport!
Alice Really? What sport do you do at school?
Mark I play football, but I'm not very good at it and I hate it!
Alice How often do you play it?
Mark Only once a week, thank goodness!
We play it on Friday afternoons – I hate Friday!

> ### Extra activity 1
> - In pairs, students can act out the dialogue between Mark and Alice, using the questions and answers in exercise 3 as a guide.
> - Encourage them to use correct intonation and to sound enthusiastic.
> - Check that they are using the correct subject pronouns.

Speaking

Aim

To ask and answer questions about sports

Warm-up

- Ask students what their favourite sports are. If they don't like sports, ask them what they prefer to do.

Exercise 4 Pairwork

- Students read and think about the questions.
- In pairs, students exchange information about their favourite sports. Monitor and make sure students are making a note of their partner's answers and that they swap roles.
- Make a note of any repeated errors to check at the end of the lesson.
- Ask one or two pairs to report back to the class.

ANSWERS
Students' own answers.

Extra activity 1

- In pairs, students think of a famous sports star. Their partner asks questions to guess who it is, e.g. S1: *Does he / she play football?* S2: *Yes, he / she does. / No, he / she doesn't.*

Extra activity 2

- As a whole class or in small groups, students play *Hangman* with sports words.

Writing

Aim

To write a short paragraph about your partner's favourite school day and sports

Warm-up

- Ask one or two students to tell the class about their partner's favourite school day and sports.

Exercise 5

- Students complete the paragraph with the information about their partner from exercise 4.
- Encourage students to look at the words before and after each gap and to think carefully about the words they put in each gap.
- Ask students to tell the rest of the class about their partner. Encourage them to read out their sentences.

ANSWERS
Students' own answers.

Exercise 6

- Students make notes about themselves to answer the questions in exercise 4.
- They then write a rough draft of their paragraph.
- Students swap their drafts with a partner, who corrects the mistakes.
- Students write a final draft in class or for homework.

ANSWERS
Students' own answers.

Extra activity 1

- Students can add photos of themselves doing the sports to their paragraph, or they can illustrate it.

Extra activity 2

- Put the students in two teams. Call out the names of famous sports people and ask each team to make a sentence, e.g. T: *Rafael Nadal* SS: *He plays tennis*. The team with the most correct sentences wins.

Further practice
Workbook page 89

Grammar

Present simple (affirmative, negative, interrogative, and short answers)

Adverbs of frequency

Prepositions of time

Question words

How often …? + Expressions of frequency

Object pronouns

Vocabulary

Daily routines

Sports

Review B page 46

Vocabulary

Exercise 1

ANSWERS

2 I have breakfast.
3 I go to school.
4 I have lunch.
5 I get home.
6 I have dinner.
7 I go to bed.

Exercise 2

ANSWERS

1 cycling   2 athletics   3 swimming   4 basketball
5 tennis

Grammar

Exercise 3

ANSWERS

1 Mr Adams doesn't teach music. Mr Adams teaches history.
2 You don't get up at eight o'clock. You get up at seven o'clock.
3 Matt and Sandra don't live in London. Matt and Sandra live in Dublin.

Exercise 4

ANSWERS

1 always   2 usually   3 often   4 sometimes   5 rarely

Exercise 5

ANSWERS

1 on   2 at   3 in   4 at   5 at

Exercise 6

ANSWERS

1 Does Fred have a shower every morning? Yes, he does.
2 Do you like pop music? No, I don't.
3 Do Tom and Sarah go to school on Saturdays? No, they don't.

Exercise 7

ANSWERS

1 When   2 What time   3 How often   4 Where
5 What

Exercise 8

ANSWERS

1 She   2 us   3 They   4 her   5 him

My Progress

• Students read the sentences and choose the faces that are true for them.

• If students have fewer than three smiley faces, encourage them to review the grammar or vocabulary of the previous two units and do more practice.

Songs

The following songs would be appropriate to use at this point:

• *Suddenly I see* by K T Tunstall (present simple)
• *You're my best friend* by Queen (present simple)
• *Girlfriend* by Avril Lavigne (present simple)
• *For no one* by The Beatles (present simple)
• *Beat Again* by JLS (subject / object pronouns)

Culture club

Grammar

Present simple (affirmative and negative)

Question words

Prepositions of time

Object pronouns

Vocabulary

Daily routines

Topic

School and education in the UK

Culture club B   page 47

Warm-up

- Ask students to look at the photos. Ask questions, e.g. *How old do you think the girl is?* (thirteen) *What's her name?* (Rachel) *Can you name the daily routine in the second photo?* (have lunch) Ask *What is the text about?* (going to school)

Aim

To read and understand a text about school in the UK

Warm-up

- Tell students they are going to make a list of subjects they think that Rachel might study at school.
- Books closed. Give students two minutes to write down as many school subjects as they can.
- The student who has the most subjects is the winner.

Exercise 1

- Students read the text in detail and answer the questions.
- Check the answers with the class, encouraging students to give as full answers as possible.

ANSWERS

1 She wears a school uniform.
2 She starts school at 8.50 a.m. and finishes at 3.30 p.m.
3 She has seven lessons every day.
4 She likes P.E., music, I.C.T., and English.
5 She doesn't like maths and history.

> ### Extra activity
> - Play *Hangman* with school subjects.

Exercise 2 Focus on you

- Students write a letter to Rachel to tell her about their school and their school day.
- Encourage them to use Rachel's letter as a model.
- Students make notes before they do a rough draft. If students need more support, write the following headings on the board to help them: *the name of their school, the year they're in, how many lessons they have each day, uniform or no uniform, what days they go to school, start time, finish time, school subjects, what they like / don't like.*
- Students then produce a rough draft from their notes.
- They can swap drafts with a partner, who corrects the mistakes.
- Students then produce a final draft in class or for homework.

ANSWERS
Students' own answers.

> ### Extra activity
> - In pairs, students ask and answer questions about one school day in their week.
> - Give them a few minutes to prepare questions.
> - Check that students are swapping roles and using the present simple and question words correctly.
> - Ask one or two pairs to report back to the class.

Further practice
Workbook pages 80–89

5 I can sing very well

Grammar

can (ability): affirmative, negative, interrogative, and short answers

Degrees of ability (*very well, well, quite well, at all*)

Imperatives

Vocabulary

Free-time activities

Communication

Making suggestions

/ə/ /ɑː/

Intonation in phrases

Skills

Reading: Superheroes

Listening: A radio interview

Speaking: Ask and answer questions about things you can do

Writing: Free time and abilities

Topics

Multiculturalism: Hobbies and free-time activities

Presentation page 48

Aim

To present the new language in a motivating context

Story

Holly arrives late for the audition. Ruby becomes alarmed when she realizes that her uncle will not be at the auditions.

Warm-up

- Ask students what they can remember from the last part of the photo story.
- Ask students to look at the photo. Ask questions, e.g. *Who are the people?* (Jazz, Alex, Ruby, Holly, Luke, a teacher) *Which student hasn't got a school uniform?* (Ruby) *Where are they?* (In the school theatre/hall) *What can you see in the photo?* (a piano and drums).

Exercise 1 Read and listen 42

- Play the CD. Students read and listen to answer the question.
- Go through the *Check it out!* box and make sure students understand the expressions.
- Check any other unknown vocabulary in the text.
- Play the CD. Students listen and repeat chorally, then individually.

ANSWERS

b Mr Smith

Transcript Student's Book page 48

Exercise 2 Comprehension

- Individually, students correct the sentences, referring back to the dialogue in exercise 1 as necessary.
- They can compare answers in pairs.
- Check the answers with the class, encouraging students to read out the complete sentences.

ANSWERS

1 Holly arrives at the auditions late.
2 Ruby is at the auditions.
3 Mr Smith doesn't come to the auditions.

Extra activity

- In small groups, students act out the dialogue in exercise 1.

Consolidation

- Remind students to copy any new words or phrases into their vocabulary notebooks.

Language focus page 49

Aim

To practise the target language in a new context

Exercise 3 Dialogue focus

- Explain that students will be using the new language they heard in the main story dialogue in exercise 1.
- Explain the meaning of *can / can't*.
- In pairs, students read and complete the dialogues. Remind them to look back at the story on page 48.
- Students can compare answers in pairs. Do not check the answers at this point.

Exercise 4 43

- Play the CD. Students listen and check their answers to exercise 3.
- Students listen again and repeat chorally, then individually.

ANSWERS / AUDIO CD TRACK 43

1 **Mrs Lee** What **¹**can you do? Can you sing?
  Holly Yes, I **²**can. I can sing very well.
2 **Mrs Lee** **³**Can you play the guitar?
  Holly No, I **⁴**can't. I can't play the guitar at all.
3 **Luke** She can act very well.
  Jazz And she **⁵**can dance, too. She's brilliant!

Exercise 5 Focus on you

- Read the first question and ask a student to choose one of the responses. Explain that these questions and answers are used to talk about general ability to do something.
- Students read the questions and circle the correct answers for themselves.

ANSWERS

Students' own answers.

Exercise 6 Pairwork

- In pairs, students ask and answer the questions in exercise 5.
- Ask one or two pairs to read out their questions and answers for the class.

Students' own answers.

Vocabulary page 50

Free-time activities

Aims

To present and practise vocabulary for free-time activities: *go bowling, go shopping, go skateboarding, go to the cinema, play cards, play chess, play computer games, play the guitar, read comics, ride a bike, send text messages, surf the Internet*; to ask and answer about free-time activities

Warm-up

- Students look at the illustrations. Ask one or two questions about the pictures, e.g. *Can you play the guitar? Can you ride a bike?* and elicit answers. Point to the illustrations as you are asking the questions if necessary.

Exercise 1 44

- Students match the pictures with the activities. This can be done individually or as a whole class.
- Play the CD. Students listen and check their answers.
- Students listen again and repeat chorally, then individually.

ANSWERS / AUDIO CD TRACK 44
1	f	play computer games
2	k	send text messages
3	b	go skateboarding
4	l	surf the Internet
5	h	play cards
6	c	go to the cinema
7	e	play chess
8	a	go shopping
9	i	read comics
10	g	play the guitar
11	d	go bowling
12	j	ride a bike

Exercise 2

- Go through the *Look!* box with the class, pointing out how *the* is used in English with a musical instrument.
- Ask students to compare this with verbs in their own language.
- In pairs, students look at the picture of Joe's bag and decide what he does in his free time. Remind them to look back at the activities in exercise 1 if necessary.
- Students write sentences about Joe's free-time activities.
- Check the answers with the class.

ANSWERS
(in any order)
1 Joe goes skateboarding.
2 Joe reads comics.
3 Joe plays cards.
4 Joe goes to the cinema.
5 Joe plays computer games.

Exercise 3 Pairwork

- Read the example with a student.
- Explain that the students are going to ask and answer questions about free-time activities.
- Before you begin the activity, revise *How often …?* and expressions of frequency.
- In pairs, students ask and answer questions about their free-time activities.
- Monitor and check they are using the expressions from exercise 1 correctly.
- Ask one or two students to tell the class about their partner.

ANSWERS
Students' own answers.

Extra activity 1

- This can be done in small groups or as a whole class.
- Call out the activities from exercise 1 without the verb for students to give you the correct verb, e.g. T: *bowling* SS: *go*.

Extra activity 2

- This can be done in small groups or as a whole class.
- One student chooses an expression from exercise 1 and mimes it for the class / group. The other students guess which activity it is.

Consolidation

- Encourage students to make a note of the free-time activities and the notes in the *Look!* box in their vocabulary notebooks.
- Remind them of the different ways of recording vocabulary, e.g. they may want to illustrate these items instead of writing a translation.

Further practice
CD-ROM; Workbook page 91

Grammar page 51

can (ability): Affirmative and negative

Aim

To present and practise the affirmative and negative forms of *can* (ability)

Warm-up

- Write *can* and *can't* on the board. Ask students to try and remember what Holly can and can't do.

Grammar box

- Go through the grammar box with the class.
- Remind students that we use *can / can't* to talk about ability. Point out that *can* does not have a third person singular form.
- Point out the full negative form *cannot* at the bottom of the box.
- Encourage students to go back to the presentation dialogue on page 48 and to find more examples of *can* and *can't*.

Rules page 90

Exercise 1

- Students complete the sentences with *can* or *can't*.
- Remind them to look carefully at each picture before choosing their answers.
- Check the answers with the class.

ANSWERS
1 She can't sing.
2 They can dance.
3 He can't ride a bike.
4 They can play the guitar.
5 She can't play tennis.

Exercise 2

- Individually, students write sentences about what they can and can't do using the activities in exercise 1.
- They can compare sentences in pairs.
- Ask one or two pairs to feed back to the class.

ANSWERS
Students' own answers.

> **Extra activity**
> - Ask students to say what they can and can't do using some of the expressions from page 50, e.g. *I can play the guitar*.

Exercise 3 Pronunciation 45

- Explain that *can* has different sounds, and can be weak or strong. In questions and positive sentences *can* is weak /kən/. In short answers *can* is strong /kɑn/. The negative *can't* is always strong /kɑːnt/.
- Play the CD. Students listen to the two forms.
- Students listen again and repeat chorally, then individually.

Transcript Student's Book page 51

> **Extra activity**
> - Read out the sentences from exercise 1 and ask students to call out if the sound is weak or strong, e.g. T: *He can play chess.* SS: *weak*.

Exercise 4 46

- Play the CD. Students listen and choose the correct word.
- They can compare answers in pairs.
- Check the answers with the class.
- Students listen again and repeat chorally, then individually.

ANSWERS / AUDIO CD TRACK 46
Katie can't send text messages.
1 Tom can't play football.
2 I can speak English.
3 My mum can't send emails.
4 She can play the piano.
5 I can play tennis.
6 He can't act.

> **Extra activity**
> - Ask students to identify which sentences in exercise 4 have the weak /ə/ and which have the strong /ɑː/ sound (Weak: 2, 4, 5. Strong: Example sentence, 1, 3, 6)

Degrees of ability

Aim

To present and practise different degrees of ability

Warm-up

- On the board write *What can you do well?* Elicit the meaning, focusing on *well*.
- In pairs, students tell each other what they can do well.
- Ask some students to tell the class about their partners.

Grammar box

- Read through the grammar box with the class, drawing students' attention to the position of the degree expression in the middle column, and the symbols in the final column.
- Ask *Can Holly dance?* (Yes, she can) *Can she dance quite well or very well?* (Very well).

Rules page 90

Exercise 5

- Students study the table and write sentences.
- Remind them to look back at the grammar box to check the symbols if necessary.
- Check the answers with the class.

ANSWERS
1 Holly can act very well.
2 Ruby can act quite well.
3 Holly can dance quite well.
4 Ruby can't dance at all.
5 Holly can sing well.
6 Ruby can't sing at all.

Exercise 6 Game!

- Students play a memory game. One student makes a sentence beginning with *I can*. The student on their left repeats the sentence in the third person and then makes one of their own with *I can*. The next student must make the first two sentences in the third person before making a sentence of their own. The game continues until a student forgets one of the sentences and is out of the game. The last student in the game is the winner.

Finished?

- Students write three sentences about what their friends or people in their family can and can't do. Remind them to look back at the sentences in exercise 1 for useful expressions if necessary, and at the grammar box for degrees of ability.
- Ask one or two students to tell the class what their friends / family can and can't do.

ANSWERS
Students' own answers.

| Further practice
CD-ROM; Workbook page 91

Communication page 52

Making suggestions

Aim

To present and practise making suggestions

Warm-up

- Ask one or two questions about the photo, e.g. *Where do you think Sam and Emma are?* (At school) *What are they talking about?* (What to do after school).

Exercise 1 47

- Before students listen to the CD, encourage them to read the dialogue.
- Play the CD. Students read and listen.
- Students can listen only, without looking at their books, if they are confident enough.
- Check the answers with the class.
- Students listen again and repeat chorally, then individually.

ANSWERS
1 play basketball
2 play cards

Transcript   Student's Book page 52

- Explain that the expressions *Let's* in sentences and *Why don't we?* in questions are used to make suggestions.

You ask, You answer

- Read through the *You ask, You answer* box with the class.
- Make sure students are aware of which answers are for agreeing and which are for disagreeing.

Extra activity

- In pairs, students act out the dialogues in exercise 1.
- Ask one or two pairs to act them out in front of the class.

Exercise 2 Pronunciation 48

- Remind students of the falling intonation in *Wh-* questions and the rising intonation in *yes / no* questions (see Student's Book page 42).
- Play the CD. Students listen and read.
- Students listen again and repeat chorally, then individually.

Transcript   Student's Book page 52

Extra activity 1

- If you feel students need more practice in question intonation, read the questions from the pronunciation exercise from the end for students to repeat chorally, then individually, e.g. *tennis?, play tennis?, we play tennis?, don't we play tennis?, Why don't we play tennis?*

Extra activity 2

- Write the longer dialogue from exercise 1 on the board.
- Ask a pair of students to read it out.
- Rub out one of the sentences and ask a different pair to read the dialogue, saying the missing sentence.
- Continue in this way until you have rubbed out the whole dialogue and students can say it from memory.

Exercise 3 Pairwork

- Students write conversations about free-time activities.
- Remind them to use the activities in the box and to look back at the *You ask, You answer* box if necessary.
- In pairs, students practise their dialogues.
- Ask one or two students to act out their dialogues in front of the class.

ANSWERS
Students' own answers.

| Further practice
CD-ROM; Workbook page 93

Grammar page 53

can (ability): Interrogative and short answers

Aim

To present and practise *can* interrogative and short answers

Warm-up

- Ask questions, e.g. *Can Holly sing? Can Ruby act? Can Holly play the guitar?* Elicit *yes / no* answers.
- Write the questions on the board. Based on students' answers, write *Yes, she _____. No, she _____.* etc. See if the students can complete the short answers correctly.

Grammar box

- Read through the grammar box with the class.
- Draw students' attention to the change in word order for the interrogative form. Remind them that *can* does not have a third person singular form.
- Remind students that *can* has two sounds, and can be weak or strong. In questions and positive sentences *can* is weak /kən/. In short answers *can* is strong /kɑn/. The negative *can't* is always strong /kɑːnt/.

Rules page 90

Exercise 1

- Students complete the dialogue with *can* or *can't*.
- Remind them to read the whole dialogue first.
- Students can compare answers in pairs.
- Check the answers with the class.

ANSWERS
1 can't 2 Can 3 can 4 Can 5 can

> ### Extra activity
> - In pairs, students act out the dialogue in exercise 1.
> - Stronger students can change the abilities.

Exercise 2

- Students write questions using the prompts. Then they answer the questions using the information in the table.
- They can compare answers in pairs.
- Check the answers with the class, asking students to read out their answers.

ANSWERS
1 Can Kate ski? Yes, she can.
2 Can Rob and Kevin ski? No, they can't.
3 Can Kate ride a bike? No, she can't.
4 Can Rob, Kate, and Kevin swim? Yes, they can.
5 Can Rob play football? Yes, he can.
6 Can Kevin play football? No, he can't.

> ### Extra activity 2
> - Give students two minutes to look at the table in exercise 2.
> - Books closed. Ask questions and elicit the correct answers from the class, e.g. T: *Can Rob swim?* SS: *Yes, he can.*
> - This can also be done in pairs with one student asking the questions and the other giving the answers.

Exercise 3 Game!

- Go through the example dialogue, making sure students understand how the activity works.
- In pairs, students ask and answer questions about the things in the box.
- Monitor and check that they are forming questions and short answers correctly.
- The first pair to answer everything are the winners.

ANSWERS
Students' own answers.

Imperatives

Aim

To present and practise affirmative and negative imperatives

Warm-up

- On the board write *Stop! Go!* and *Sit down!* Ask what the sentences are (commands). Explain that the structure used to give commands is called the imperative. Point out that subject pronouns are not used in imperatives.

Grammar box

- Go through the grammar box with the class.
- Draw students' attention to the use of the auxiliary *don't* in negative imperatives.
- Point out that the main verb is always in the infinitive form.

Rules page 90

Exercise 4

- Students complete the sentences with the affirmative and negative imperatives.
- Explain the tick (✓) for affirmative and cross (✗) for negative.
- Check the answers with the class.

ANSWERS
1 Listen 2 Don't send 3 Sit down 4 Speak
5 Don't be 6 Don't play

> ### Extra activity
> - Play the game Simon Says (see Teacher's Book page 9) with simple affirmative and negative imperatives of classroom language, e.g. *Simon says stand up!, Don't sit down!, Simon says touch your head!*

Finished?

- Students write three more questions with *can*.
- In pairs, students ask and answer their questions. Check that they are using the forms correctly. Make a note of any repeated errors to check at the end of the lesson.
- Ask one or two pairs to tell the class about their partner.

Students' own answers.

> ## Consolidation
> - Encourage students to make a note of the grammar boxes, examples, and rules in their grammar notebooks.

Further practice
CD-ROM; Workbook page 92

Skills   pages 54–55

Reading

Aim
To read and understand a letters page in a magazine

Warm-up
- Ask *Do you know these superheroes?* (Batman, Superman, Spiderman) *Do you know the films they are in?*

> ## Background notes
> - Superman is a fictional comic book superhero character, who first appeared in 1938. He was born on the planet Krypton and was a hero in the town of Metropolis. He works in disguise as a reporter called Clark Kent on *The Daily Planet* newspaper. The 1978 film starred Christopher Reeve in the role of Superman.
> - *Smallville* is an American TV series based on the early life of the Superman character. There have been several series and it stars Tom Welling as Clark Kent.
> - Batman is a fictional comic book superhero, who first appeared in 1939. He is often referred to as The Dark Knight or The Caped Crusader. Batman lives in the fictional American city of Gotham City. His main enemy is The Joker. Batman has featured in many films. In the 2008 film *The Dark Knight*, Heath Ledger played The Joker, but sadly died before the film was released.
> - Spider-Man is a fictional American comic book superhero character, who first appeared in 1962. Spider-Man is a teenager called Peter Parker, who has super strength and agility. He can shoot spider webs from his wrists (web-shooters) and to cling on and swing between buildings. The first Spider-Man film was released in 2002 and starred Tobey Maguire and Kirsten Dunst.

Exercise 1
- Ask students to look at the example and to find the information in the text.
- Individually or in pairs, students read the text again and answer the questions and correct any false sentences.
- Check the answers with the class. Encourage stronger students to give more detail for the true answers.

1 True.   2 False. He can't fly. He can run fast.   3 False. He can climb buildings.   4 False. He can fly.   5 True. He has X-ray vision.   6 False. Superman's real name is Clark Kent.

> ## Extra activity
> - Students choose a superhero of their own choice and write four true / false sentences about them. They swap with a partner who identifies the false sentences.

Listening

Aim
To listen and understand a radio interview about free-time activities

Warm-up
- Ask students to look at the photo of the comics and ask *Do you know any of these comics? Do you read comics?*

Exercise 2 ☺ 49
- Before students listen to the CD, encourage them to read the answer options.
- Play the CD. Students listen and choose the correct answers. Play the CD again if necessary.
- Check the answers with the class.

1 has   2 often   3 American   4 Batman
5 is intelligent   6 really likes

Sally Hello, Sally here. Today we're talking about free-time activities. Let's welcome Nick to the studio. Hi Nick, how are you?
Nick Hello, Sally.
Sally Nick, tell us about your hobbies. What do you do in your free time?
Nick I have lots of hobbies. I love sport, especially basketball. But a lot of the time, I stay at home and I read my comics, or I watch TV or DVDs.
Sally Comics? That's interesting. What comics do you read?
Nick Well, I love Japanese comics, but my favourites are old American comics. I love the Batman comics.
Sally Really? That's interesting.
Nick Yes, Batman's my favourite superhero.
Sally Why is he special?
Nick Well, he doesn't have any superpowers.
Sally Can he fly?
Nick No, he can't fly like Superman, and he can't jump onto tall buildings like Spider-Man, but he's amazing!
Sally Why do you like him?
Nick He's very strong and intelligent, and helps to protect his city, Gotham City, against The Joker.
Sally Do you like the Batman films?
Nick Yes, I do. I love all the films, but my favourite film's *The Dark Knight*. Christian Bale is Batman and he's fantastic.
Sally Great. I can't wait to watch it! Thanks, Nick!

> ## Extra activity
> - In small groups or as a whole class, students choose a superhero and mime his / her special powers. The others guess who it is.

Speaking

Aim

To ask and answer about activities you can and can't do

Warm-up

- Ask students one or two free-time activity questions, e.g. *Can you play basketball?*, *Can you play the piano?*, etc.

Exercise 3

- Students read the list of activities and decide if they can or can't do them. They complete the *Me* column in the table.

ANSWERS
Students' own answers.

Exercise 4 Pairwork

- In pairs, students ask and answer questions to complete the *My partner* column in the table in exercise 3.
- Monitor and check that students are using the correct question and answer forms, and refer them back to the grammar box on page 53 if necessary.
- Make a note of any repeated errors to check at the end of the lesson.
- Ask one or two pairs to tell the rest of the class about what their partner can and can't do.

ANSWERS
Students' own answers.

> ### Extra activity
> - In small groups or as a class, students use the information they have found and make a graph to represent the number of students in the class who can and can't do each activity. This can be displayed on the classroom wall.

Writing

Aim

To write a short paragraph about what you do in your free time, and your abilities

Warm-up

- Ask students one or two questions about what they do after school each day, e.g. *Do you ride your bike after school? Do you surf the Internet every day? How often do you go swimming?* Elicit answers, and review adverbs of frequency and expressions of frequency.

Exercise 5

- Individually, students read the information and complete the paragraph about Ellie.
- Remind them to look back at the grammar box on page 51 to review degrees of ability if necessary.
- Tell them there is one gap which does not need a word (gap 2).
- Students can compare answers in pairs.
- Check the answers with the class.

ANSWERS
1 play 2 – 3 watch 4 read 5 well 6 surf
7 meet friends 8 shopping

> ### Extra activity 1
> - Ask students some comprehension questions about the paragraph in exercise 5, e.g. *How often does Ellie play tennis?* (Twice a week) *What does she do in the evenings?* (She watches TV, reads a book, surfs the Internet) *Can she use computers?* (Yes, she can use a computer very well), etc.

> ### Extra activity 2
> - Give students a few minutes to look at the information about Ellie.
> - Books closed. Ask students comprehension questions (see above) and see how much they can remember.

Exercise 6

- Students make notes on what they do in their free time, and their abilities. Remind them to look at the grammar boxes on page 51 if necessary and to refer to the information about Ellie in exercise 5.
- Students use their notes to write a first draft of their paragraph.
- Encourage them to use degrees of ability in their paragraph.
- They can swap paragraphs with a partner, who corrects the mistakes.
- Make a note of any repeated errors and check them with the class before students write a final draft.
- Students can produce a final draft for homework or in class.

ANSWERS
Students' own answers.

> ### Extra activity 1
> - If students complete their final draft for homework, they can add illustrations to it.

> ### Extra activity 2
> - Students imagine what their favourite superhero does during the day and in the evenings. They write a short paragraph using the model in exercise 5.

Further practice
Workbook page 94

6 What's she doing now?

Grammar
Present continuous (affirmative, spelling variations, negative, interrogative and short answers)

Question words + present continuous

Vocabulary
Clothes

Communication
Money and shopping for clothes

/iː/ /i/

Skills
Reading: Let's Go! Summer Camp

Listening: A telephone conversation

Speaking: Describe what people are doing

Writing: A postcard from your holiday

Topics
Multiculturalism: Travel

Presentation   page 56

Aim
To present the new language in a motivating context

Story
Ruby and Holly are doing the auditions for the school musical. Ruby's audition does not go very well and Holly's goes very well. Holly gets the part of Suzannah in the school musical. Her friends are very happy.

Warm-up
- Ask students what they can remember from the last part of the photo story.
- Ask one or two questions about the main photo, e.g. *Who's on the stage?* (Ruby) *Who else is there?* (Holly, Jazz, Luke, and Alex)

Exercise 1 Read and listen 50
- Before they listen, ask students to predict who they think gets the part.
- Play the CD. Students read and listen.
- Stronger students can listen without reading their books.
- Check the answers with the class.
- Check students have understood the dialogue. Refer them to the *Check it out!* box and explain the phrases.
- Check any other unknown vocabulary in the text.
- Play the CD. Students listen again and repeat chorally, then individually.

ANSWER

a Holly

Transcript   Student's Book page 56

Exercise 2 Comprehension
- Individually or in pairs, students complete the sentences with the correct name. Remind them to look back at the dialogue in exercise 1 if necessary.
- Check the answers with the class, asking students to read out their completed sentences.

ANSWERS

1 Ruby 2 Holly 3 Ruby 4 Ruby 5 Holly

Extra activity
- In small groups, students act out the dialogue.

Consolidation
- Remind students to copy the words and phrases into their vocabulary notebooks.

Language focus   page 57

Aim
To review and practise the new language in context

Exercise 3 Dialogue focus
- Students read and match the dialogues with the photos.
- Remind them that the dialogues are the same as the dialogue they read in exercise 1.
- Students can compare answers in pairs. Do not check answers at this point.

Exercise 4 51
- Play the CD. Students listen and check their answers to exercise 3.
- Students listen again and repeat chorally, then individually.

Transcript   Student's Book page 57

ANSWERS

2 b 3 a

Extra activity
- In small groups, students act out the dialogues.

Exercise 5 Focus on you
- Write the example on the board and ask students to find and underline it in the dialogue in exercise 1.
- In pairs, students write dialogues using the words in the box.

ANSWERS

Students' own answers.

Exercise 6 Pairwork

- In pairs, students practise their dialogues from exercise 5.
- Students can swap pairs.
- Ask one or two pairs to act out their dialogues in front of the class.

ANSWERS
Students' own answers.

Vocabulary page 58

Clothes

Aim

To present and practise clothes vocabulary: *cap, dress, jacket, jumper, shirt, shoes, shorts, skirt, top, trainers, trousers, T-shirt;* to review colours

Warm-up

- Ask one or two questions about what you and students are wearing today, e.g. *What colour is this?* (Point to an item of your clothing)*What colour is Mario's T-shirt?* (Point to the student's piece of clothing) Avoid asking questions with the present continuous at this point.

Exercise 1 52

- Ask students to look at the pictures and see how many words for clothes they know.
- Individually or in pairs, students match the pictures with the words in the box.
- Play the CD. Students listen and check their answers.
- Students listen again and repeat chorally, then individually.

ANSWERS / AUDIO CD TRACK 52
1 cap   2 jumper   3 top   4 trousers   5 shirt   6 skirt
7 shorts   8 shoes   9 trainers   10 jacket   11 T-shirt
12 dress

Extra activity

- Give students a few minutes to look at the pictures and the numbers again.
- Books closed. Call out a number and see if students can remember which item of clothing it is.
- This could be done in small groups and the group with most correct answers is the winner.

Exercise 2 Pairwork

- In pairs, students ask and answer about the colour of the clothes in exercise 1.
- Monitor and check that students are using singular and plural forms of *be* correctly, and do a quick review if necessary.
- Stronger students can do this with their books closed.

ANSWERS
Students' own answers.

Extra activity

- In small groups, a student chooses an item from exercise 1 and starts to draw it on a piece of paper. The others guess what it is. The student who guesses correctly draws the next item of clothing.
- The group which guesses the most items correctly in two minutes is the winner.

Exercise 3

- Students complete the crossword with the missing letters.
- Remind them to count the number of letters in each word and the spaces available before they begin to write.

ANSWERS
1 shirt   2 T-shirt   3 top   4 jumper   5 shoes   6 dress
7 shorts   8 skirt
Mystery word: trousers

Exercise 4

- Go through the *Look!* box with the class. Ask students what the difference is between English and their language.
- Remind students that adjectives always go before the noun in English.
- Remind students too that adjectives and colours do not agree with the noun in English: they stay the same whether the noun is singular or plural.
- Pre-teach the phrase *I'm wearing …*
- Students write about what they are wearing. Remind them to write about the colour of what they are wearing too.
- Monitor and check that students are using colour adjectives correctly.
- Students can swap sentences with a partner who corrects any mistakes.

ANSWERS
Students' own answers.

Extra activity 1

- Collect in students' sentences from exercise 4 and give them out to a different student.
- Ask students to read out the description they have for the others to guess who it is.

Extra activity 2

- Students can look back at the photo on page 56 and describe what the students are wearing.

Consolidation

- Remind students to make a note of the vocabulary in their vocabulary notebooks. They may find it useful to draw a small picture beside each word rather than write a translation.

| Further practice
CD-ROM; Workbook page 96

Grammar page 59

Present continuous (Affirmative)

Aim

To present and practise the present continuous affirmative

Warm-up

- Say true sentences about yourself, e.g. *I'm wearing trousers. I'm standing up.* Write them on the board.
- Ask students if the sentences describe things which are happening now or things that always happen.
- Circle the auxiliary verb *be* and the *-ing* forms in the sentences and explain that the structure is called the present continuous. Explain that the present continuous is used to describe things which are happening now.

Grammar box

- Go through the grammar box with the class, pointing out the use of the verb *be* and the *-ing* form.

Rules page 95

Exercise 1

- Students complete the sentences with the affirmative form of the present continuous.
- Check the answers with the class.

ANSWERS
1 'm going   2 're studying   3 're doing
4 's wearing   5 're watching   6 's raining

Spelling variations – *-ing* form

Grammar box

- Go through the grammar box as a class, pointing out how the infinitives change when *-ing* is added.
- Refer students to the spelling rules on page 95.

Rules page 95

> **Extra activity**
> - Books closed. Write verbs in the *-ing* form on the board. Spell some correctly and others incorrectly. Students say which are incorrectly spelt, and correct them.

Exercise 2

- Students write sentences using the prompts.
- Tell them to use short forms and to look back at the grammar box if necessary.
- Check the answers with the class.

ANSWERS
1 You're writing an email.
2 I'm having a shower.
3 My mum's reading a book.
4 Mark's getting up now.
5 They're sitting in the garden.
6 Hannah's dancing in her bedroom.

> **Extra activity**
> - Call out the infinitive form of some verbs and ask students to spell the *-ing* form, e.g. *sit, swim, run, write,* etc.

Exercise 3 Game!

- Sit students in two circles to play the memory game.
- One student in each circle begins by adding an activity to the last sentence of the example.
- The student on his / her left does the same.
- The game continues until one student forgets an activity and is out of the game. The last student left is the winner.

Present continuous (Negative)

Aim

To present and practise the present continuous negative

Warm-up

- Say an affirmative and a negative sentence about yourself to the class, e.g. *I'm wearing a blue shirt. I'm not wearing a red shirt.* Write the sentences on the board.
- Ask a student to underline the negative form.

Grammar box

- Go through the grammar box with the class. Remind students of the negative form of *be* if necessary.
- Practise the pronunciation of the sentences in the box.

Rules page 95

Exercise 4

- Students rewrite the sentences using the prompts.
- Make sure they are using the affirmative and negative forms correctly.
- Check the answers with the class. Ask students to read out their complete sentences, spelling the *-ing* forms.

ANSWERS
1 We aren't going to the shops. We're going to the cinema.
2 She isn't watching TV. She's listening to her MP3 player.
3 They aren't studying maths. They're studying history.
4 I'm not reading a book. I'm having lunch.
5 He isn't doing karate. He's playing basketball.

Finished?

- Students write sentences about three people using affirmative and negative forms of the present continuous.
- Check that students are spelling the *-ing* forms correctly.

> **Extra activity**
> - In small groups or as a class, a student mimes some of the daily routines (Unit 3), sports (Unit 4), or free-time activities (Unit 5).
> - The others guess what the action is using the present continuous. The student who guesses correctly mimes next.

> **Consolidation**
> - Encourage students to make a note of the grammar in their grammar notebooks and to write example sentences of their own.

Further practice
CD-ROM; Workbook pages 96–97

Communication page 60

Money and shopping for clothes

Aims

To present and practise prices in English; to present and practise language for shopping for clothes

Warm-up

- Write the money symbol £ and letter *p* on the board. Elicit their names in English (pound and 'p' / pence).

Exercise 1 Pronunciation 🎧 53

- Read through the numbers as a class and see if students can hear the difference in the sounds.
- Play the CD. Students listen.
- Students listen again and repeat chorally, then individually.

Transcript Student's Book page 60

Exercise 2 🎧 54

- Play the CD. Students listen and identify the price they hear.
- Students listen again and check their answers.
- Students listen again and repeat chorally, then individually.

ANSWERS / AUDIO CD TRACK 54
1 b   2 b   3 a   4 a
1 Forty pounds
2 Sixty pounds
3 Nineteen pounds ninety-nine
4 Thirteen pounds thirty

> #### Extra activity
> - If students need more practice, call out more -*teen* and -*ty* numbers for students to say which sound they hear, /tiːn/ or /ti/.

Exercise 3 🎧 55

- Students read through the dialogue quickly before they listen.
- Play the CD. Students listen and choose the correct answers.
- Check the answers with the class.
- Play the CD again. Students listen again and repeat chorally, then individually.

Transcript Student's Book page 60

ANSWERS
1
1 T-shirt   2 £10.99   3 medium
2
1 trousers   2 £39.99   3 small   4 small   5 medium
6 leave

You ask, You answer

- Go through the *You ask, You answer* box with the class.
- In pairs, students take turns to ask and answers questions from the box.

> #### Extra activity
> - Give students a few minutes to read the dialogue in exercise 3 again.
> - Books closed. Ask students questions about the dialogue and see how much they can remember about Helen and Rick, e.g. *What does Helen try on?* (a T-shirt) *What size is she?* (medium) *What size is Rick?* (small), etc.

Exercise 4 Pairwork

- Students write a new dialogue, changing the words in bold in exercise 3.
- Monitor and check that students are changing the correct words and remind them to look at the *You ask, You answer* box if necessary.
- In pairs, students practise their dialogues. Remind them to swap roles.
- Ask one or two pairs to act their dialogues out in front of the class.

ANSWERS
Students' own answers.

> #### Extra activity 1
> - Students memorize one of their dialogues in exercise 4 and act it out for the class.

> #### Extra activity 2
> - Write prices on the board in numbers and ask students to spell them as words.

> #### Consolidation
> - Encourage students to copy any new words or expressions from the lesson into their vocabulary books.

Further practice
CD-ROM; Workbook page 98

Grammar page 61

Present continuous (Interrogative and short answers)

Aim

To present and practise the present continuous interrogative and short answers

Warm-up

- Play *Hangman* to revise spelling variations of *-ing* forms.
- Revise how present continuous sentences are constructed.

Grammar box

- Go through the grammar boxes with the class. Draw students' attention to word order in questions and the fact that we do not repeat the main verb in short answers.

Rules page 95

Exercise 1

- Students write questions and short answers using the prompts.
- Monitor and check that students are spelling the *-ing* form correctly and are not repeating the main verb in the short answers.
- Make a note of any repeated errors to check at the end of the lesson.
- Check the answers with the class, asking students to read out their questions and answers.

ANSWERS
1 Is Mark watching TV? Yes, he is.
2 Are the students doing their homework? Yes, they are.
3 Is Dad having breakfast? No, he isn't.
4 Is it raining? Yes, it is.
5 Are Paul and Jenny meeting their friends? No, they aren't.
6 Is the boy running? Yes, he is.

Exercise 2 Game!

- In pairs, students choose an activity and mime it. Their partner asks questions to guess what they are doing.
- Monitor and check that students are taking turns to mime and guess, and that they are using the present continuous questions and short answers correctly.

ANSWERS
Students' own answers.

Question words + present continuous

Aim

To present and practise question words with the present continuous

Warm-up

- Revise the meanings of question words.
- Ask the students a few *Wh-* questions in the present continuous. Ask them to reply with full sentences if they can. Ask a few stronger students to try and construct a *Wh-* question in the present continuous.

Grammar box

- Go through the grammar box with the class. Focus students' attention on the question words and the order of words after them.
- Ask why there are different forms of the verb *be* in each question (They match the different subject pronouns).

Rules page 95

Exercise 3

- Students write present continuous questions and answers about the pictures.
- Check the answers with the class. Ask one student to read out their question and a different student to read out their answer.

ANSWERS
2 What are they playing? They're playing cricket.
3 Where is she going? She's going to school.
4 What is he wearing? He's wearing a T-shirt, a shirt, shorts, and a cap.

Extra activity 1

- Give students a few minutes to look at the pictures and at their questions and answers to exercise 3.
- Books closed. Call out a number from exercise 3 for a student to give you the question and another to give you the answer.

Extra activity 2

- Show students some pictures from magazines in which people are doing different things.
- Elicit what the people are doing.
- Give the pictures to the students. In pairs, they ask and answer questions about what the people are doing.

Finished?

- In pairs, students look back at the photo on page 56 and write five questions using the present continuous.
- They swap questions with their partner and answer them using the present continuous.

ANSWERS
Students' own answers.

Consolidation

- Remind students to make a note of the grammar and to write their own examples from this lesson in their grammar notebooks.

Further practice
Workbook page 97

Skills pages 62–63

Reading

Aim

To read and understand a website and an email

Warm-up

- Ask students to look at the photos and ask them one or two questions, e.g. *What are the students doing?* (They are making / decorating a mosaic. They are climbing).

Background notes

- Residential summer camps for children are very popular in the UK. Children can attend the camps without their families, and enjoy a wide range of indoor and outdoor activities including sports, music, dance, and film-making.

Exercise 1

- Ask students to read the email quickly and find out who Danny is at the camp with (Ethan, Lucy, David, and Sally).
- Students read the texts again individually and answer the questions.
- Check any unknown vocabulary with the class.
- Check the answers with the class.

ANSWERS

1 It's in Scotland.
2 It's open in July and August.
3 He's writing emails.
4 Yes, he does.
5 She's talking to an Italian boy.
6 Ethan and David are playing football.
   Sally is sunbathing.

> **Extra activity**
> - Write the words *Let's go! Summer Camp* on the board.
> - Give students two minutes to see how many other words they can make from the letters in the four words.
> - The student with the most words is the winner.

Listening

Aim

To listen to and understand a conversation between two friends about holiday activities

Warm-up

- Ask students one or two questions about holidays, e.g. *Where do you usually go on holiday? Who do you go with? Do you prefer to stay at home? What do you do on holiday?*

Exercise 2 56

- Ask students to read the sentences before they listen, focusing on the underlined words which they have to correct.
- Play the CD. Students listen and correct the underlined information.
- They can compare their answers in pairs.
- Check the answers with the class, asking students to read out the corrected parts of the dialogue.

ANSWERS / AUDIO CD TRACK 56

1 fantastic   2 France   3 boring   4 football
5 computer centre   6 can't sing at all / sounds terrible

Danny Hi, Jenny. It's Danny. How are you?
Jenny Oh, hi, Danny. I'm fine! And you?
Danny I'm fine. I'm at the Let's Go! Summer Camp. I'm having a fantastic time. Where are you?
Jenny I'm on holiday with my parents in France. We're staying at a hotel in the mountains. It's so boring!
Danny Oh no! Well, we're having a great time here, thank goodness.
Jenny Who are you with?
Danny I'm with Ethan, David, and Lucy.
Jenny What are you all doing?
Danny Ethan's playing football. He thinks he's Ronaldinho! David's in the computer centre. He's writing emails.
Jenny A computer centre! Wow!
Danny Yes, it's excellent.
Jenny What's that? It's terrible!
Danny Oh, that's Lucy! She's practising for the Pop Idol contest … She thinks she's great!
Jenny Oh dear. She sounds terrible!

> **Extra activity**
> - Play the CD. Students listen to the conversation between Danny and Jenny again.
> - In pairs, students write and act out the conversation using the sentences in exercise 2 as a guide.
> - If students are confident enough, they could act out the conversation without reading what they have written.

Speaking

Aim

To ask and answer about holiday activities using the present continuous

Warm-up

- Students look at the picture. Ask *Do you do these things on holiday? What is your favourite holiday activity?*

Exercise 3 Pairwork

- In pairs, students take turns to ask and answer about what the people in the picture are doing.
- Monitor and check for the correct use of present continuous questions and answers, and make a note of any repeated errors to check at the end of the lesson.
- Ask one or two more confident pairs to tell the class what the people are doing.

ANSWERS

(in any order)

1 What's Mrs Lipton doing? She's sunbathing.
2 What are Ryan and George doing? They're swimming.
3 What's Harvey doing? He's writing a postcard.
4 What's Hannah doing? She's making a sandcastle.
5 What are Joseph and Emily doing? They're playing volleyball.

Extra activity 1

- Stronger students can give a description of the whole picture using the present continuous.

Extra activity 2

- Give students a few minutes to look at the picture and memorize what the people are doing.
- Books closed. Ask questions about the people and see who can remember the most correct information.

Writing

Aim

To write a postcard from a holiday

Warm-up

- Ask students one or two questions about holidays, e.g. *Do you send postcards when you are on holiday? Who do you send them to? What do you write?*

Exercise 4

- Individually, students look at the picture in exercise 3 again and complete Harvey's postcard.
- They can compare answers in pairs.
- Check the answers with the class, making sure that students have spelt the *-ing* forms correctly.

ANSWERS

1 's sunbathing
2 are playing volleyball
3 are swimming
4 's making a sandcastle
5 I'm writing

Exercise 5

- Students imagine they are on holiday with their family. They make notes for a postcard on what each person in their family is doing.
- Students swap notes with a partner, who corrects any mistakes.
- Make a note of any repeated errors to check at the end of the lesson.
- Students then write a first draft of their postcard.
- Students can write a final version in class or for homework. If you have some blank postcards, give them out to students to produce their final version.
- You may find it useful to review the layout of a postcard at this point. The address goes on the right-hand side and the stamp in the top right-hand corner. Remind students of the different ways of signing off too, e.g. *See you soon, Bye for now*, etc.

ANSWERS

Students' own answers.

Further practice

Workbook page 99

| **Grammar** |
| can (ability): affirmative, negative, interrogative, short answers |
| Imperatives |
| Present continuous: affirmative, negative, short answers, and information questions |

| **Vocabulary** |
| Free-time activities |
| Clothes |

Review C   page 64

Vocabulary

Exercise 1

ANSWERS
go bowling
read comics
go shopping
ride a bike
play the guitar
send text messages

Exercise 2

ANSWERS
1 shirt   2 jacket   3 shoes   4 trousers   5 jumper
6 trainers

Grammar

Exercise 3

ANSWERS
can do
can't speak
can play
can't send

Exercise 4

ANSWERS
Can your best friend dance?
Can you skateboard?
Can your teacher speak Chinese?
Students' own answers.

Exercise 5

ANSWERS
1 Look   2 Don't watch   3 Listen   4 Don't eat

Exercise 6

ANSWERS
She's wearing a green dress.
They aren't listening to the teacher.
You're sitting in my chair!

Exercise 7

ANSWERS
Where are they going?
What are they drinking?
Who are you talking to?

My Progress

- Students read the sentences and choose the faces that are true for them.
- If students have fewer than three smiley faces, encourage them to review the grammar or vocabulary of the previous two units and do more practice.

Songs

- The following songs would be appropriate to use at this point:
- *The Greatest Day* by Take That (*can* and imperatives)
- *Angels* by Robbie Williams (present simple, present continuous)
- *The Climb* by Miley Cyrus (present continuous)
- *Spider-man* by the Ramones (Superheroes topic and present simple)
- *Don't look back in anger* by Oasis (imperatives)
- *Holiday* by Atomic Kitten (holiday theme)

Culture club

Grammar
Present simple: affirmative, negative, information questions
Adverbs of frequency

Vocabulary
Free-time activities
Prices and money

Vocabulary
Multiculturalism: Free-time activities

Culture club C page 65

Warm-up
- Ask students to look at the title and the photos and ask questions, e.g. *What is the text about? How old are the students?* (Thirteen or fourteen) *What do you think they like doing?* (Cooking, surfing the Internet) *What do you think of the activities?*

Aim
To read and understand a text about teenage life and free-time activities in the UK

> **Extra activity**
> - Books closed, students make a list of the activities they think will be mentioned in the text. Elicit their ideas and write them on the board.

Exercise 1
- Individually, students read the text and answer the questions.
- Remind them to read the questions first and to focus on the information they need to find to answer them.
- Students can compare answers in pairs.
- Check the answers with the class, encouraging students to give as much detail as possible from the text.

ANSWERS
1 They watch TV, play electronic games, and surf the Internet.
2 The clubs are usually free.
3 Boys' favourite sports are football and skateboarding.
4 He makes pizzas, biscuits, and other things.
5 She likes it because it's really interesting.

> **Extra activity**
> - In small groups, students think about the text. They discuss if they think this is the same or different for teenagers in their country.
> - Tell students to ask one person in each group to make a note of their answers.
> - Ask a spokesperson from each group to feed back to the class, encouraging students to express their views.

Exercise 2 Focus on you
- In pairs, students read the questions and brainstorm ideas for their answers.
- They answer the questions individually.

ANSWERS
Students' own answers.

> **Extra activity**
> - In small groups, students think of the perfect after-school club. They make notes about the activities and where and when it would take place.
> - Students write a mini presentation of their ideas and present them to the class.

Further practice
Workbook pages 90–99

Grammar

be: present simple

there is / there are

Vocabulary

Countries, ethnic groups, and languages

Adjectives

Project

Design an information leaflet about an ethnic group in your country

Topics

Social science: Ethnic groups, traditions, customs, and languages

Society: Respect for others

Multiculturalism: People from different countries

Curriculum extra A: Social science page 66

Warm-up

- Ask students to name some Latin American countries. Write their answers on the board or ask students to come to the board and find them on the map.
- Ask students to look at the page and ask *What is the text about?* (the indigenous people of Latin America).
- Ask a student to read the first paragraph of the text. Write the word *groups* on the board and elicit its meaning.
- Ask students to scan the text quickly to find the different ethnic groups in the text and elicit their answers.

Background notes

- Paraguay has a population of about 6,349,000. Its capital is Asunción.
- Bolivia has a population of about 9,775,000. Its constitutional capital is Sucre and its administrative capital is La Paz.
- Argentina is the second-largest country in Latin America. It has a population of around 40,000,000. Its capital is Buenos Aires.
- Brazil is the largest country in Latin America, with a population of just over 192,000,000. Its capital is Brasília.
- Peru has a population of about 29,000,000. Its capital is Lima. The main language is Spanish, but many Peruvians speak Quechua and other native languages.
- The Andes are the world's longest continental mountain range. They run along the west coast of Latin America and are in seven countries.
- Lake Titicaca is on the border of Peru and Bolivia. It is 3,812 metres above sea level. The Javari river is on the border of Brazil and Peru. It is 870km long and meets the Amazon.
- The Galvez river is a tributary of the Javari river in Peru.
- The Maici river is in north west Brazil.

Exercise 1

- Students read the text carefully and answer the questions.
- Encourage them to use their dictionaries if necessary to check any new vocabulary.
- Check the answers with the class.

ANSWERS

1 The Guaraní are from Paraguay, Bolivia, Argentina, and Brazil.
2 The Quechua tribe are from Bolivia, in the Andes.
3 It is 'water people'.
4 The Pirahã tribe is between 10,000 and 40,000 years old.
5 They are on the Maici river.

Consolidation

- Encourage students to copy any new vocabulary into their vocabulary notebooks and to illustrate new words or to write a translation.

Extra activity

- Ask students to scan the text again to find out which ethnic group lives in the forests (the Guaraní people).
- Ask students why there are problems in the forests today and how this affects the Guaraní people.
- Ask students if they know of any government initiatives to stop the problems.
- Ask the students what people can do to help the Guaraní people. Possible ideas are recycling, using less paper, boycotting companies which support deforestation, trying to raise public awareness.

Background information

- The Guaraní people are losing their land in the forests due to deforestation. Large companies cut down trees for industry, building, or to make room for crops such as tobacco.
- The Guaraní have to live on areas of land which are too small to sustain them. They are forced to take on paid work away from their land. This is against their nomadic forest traditions. Traditionally, they find fruit and meat in the forests, as well as natural medicines. This has caused an increase in health problems and the rate of infant mortality in the Guaraní people has risen.

Project

- Students can do this in class or for homework. It can be done individually, or in pairs / small groups.
- Students research an ethnic group in their country. Encourage them to find information and to make notes for all the questions on page 66.
- Students produce their leaflets and bring them into class.
- Encourage them to share information about the ethnic group in their leaflet with the rest of the class.
- The leaflets can be displayed around the class.

Grammar

Present simple: affirmative and negative

Question words + present simple

Object pronouns

Vocabulary

Daily routines

Sports

Project

Interview your favourite sportsperson

Topics

Science: Biology

Health: Fitness through sport

Curriculum extra B: Biology page 67

Warm-up

- Draw a simple picture of the human body on the board. A stick figure will do! Draw a heart shape and a circle to show the stomach.
- Elicit any parts of the human body that students might know and make sure that they know the words *arm*, *leg*, *heart*, and *stomach*.
- Ask students in their L1 what helps us move our arms and legs, and what helps our stomach and heart to work. Elicit *muscles* in the students' L1 and pre-teach the word in English, or ask them to find it in the text.
- Ask a student to read the first paragraph of the text. Tell students to find phrases in the first paragraph that match the activities in the photos (*get up, play computer games, play sports*).

Extra activity

- Ask students what we can do to keep our muscles strong and elicit the word *sport* in English.
- Write anagrams of the sports learned in Unit 4 on the board for the students to solve. Put the class into groups to solve the anagrams. The first group to solve them all is the winner.

Exercise 1

- Individually, students read the text carefully and answer the questions.
- Encourage students to use their dictionaries if necessary.
- They can compare answers in pairs.
- Check the answers with the class.

ANSWERS

1 Muscles help you to do everything.
2 Skeletal muscles help your body to move.
3 Smooth muscles help you to eat.
4 It is good to exercise for 30–60 minutes every day.
5 This is important because cold muscles don't work well.

Extra activity: *Simon says*

- Give students simple instructions to mime sports or daily routines which will use their muscles. If you say *Simon says* before the instruction, students must follow it; if you don't say *Simon says*, students must not follow your instruction, e.g. T: *Simon says 'Play tennis!'* (students mime playing tennis) T: *Have a shower* (student should not mime having a shower).
- Continue until there is only one student left.

Consolidation

- Encourage students to copy any new vocabulary into their vocabulary notebooks and to illustrate new words or to write a translation.

Extra activity

- In pairs, students ask and answer questions about the amount of exercise they do, and how often they do it. Students should use question words and the present simple for the activity.
- Check that they are taking turns to ask and answer, and that they are using the present simple and question words correctly.
- Make a note of any repeated errors to check at the end of the lesson.
- Students should make a note of their partner's answers.
- Ask some students to report back to the class about their partners.
- Do a classroom poll to find out what the most popular form of exercise is in the class.

Project

- Students can do this individually in class or for homework.
- Students think about their favourite sportsperson and make notes to answer the questions on page 67.
- Encourage them to think of other questions they could ask, e.g. *What time do you get up in the morning? What do you have for breakfast / lunch / dinner? What time do you go to bed?*
- Students produce a rough draft of their questions and their favourite sportsperson's answers from their notes.
- They can swap drafts with a partner, who corrects any mistakes.
- Students produce a final version of the interview.
- They could add photos and make it like a magazine interview or they can act it out with a partner in front of the class.

Grammar
Present simple

can

Vocabulary
Clothes

Project
Design a poster about traditional clothes in your country

Topics
History: Traditional clothes

Multiculturalism: Clothes from other countries

Curriculum extra C: History page 68

Warm-up
- Focus attention on the photos and ask students one or two questions, e.g. *Where are the people from?* (Japan and Peru) *What is special about their clothes?* (They're traditional clothes from their countries) *What clothes are the Japanese women wearing?* (Dresses) *What is the Peruvian woman wearing?* (A skirt, a jumper / jacket, and a hat /cap).

Background notes
- Japan is an island country in East Asia with a population of about 128 million. The four biggest islands in Japan are: Honshū, Hokkaidō, Kyūshū, and Shikoku. The capital, Tokyo, is located on the island of Honshū. Japan has an active volcano: Mount Fuji.
- Peru has a population of about 29,000,000. Its capital is Lima. The main language is Spanish, but many Peruvians speak Quechua and other native languages.
- Lake Titicaca is on the border of Peru and Bolivia. It is 3,812 metres above sea level.

Extra activity 1
- Play *Hangman* to revise clothes vocabulary.

Extra activity 2
- In pairs, students ask each other *What am I wearing?* and answer by describing their partner's clothes. They should include the colour of the clothes in their answer, e.g. *You're wearing a blue skirt and …* . If all the students are wearing the same school uniform, the activity could be varied by picking characters in the photo story in the Student's Book and describing what they are wearing.

Exercise 1
- Students read the text in detail and answer the questions individually.
- Encourage them to use their dictionaries to check any new vocabulary.
- Check the answers with the class.

ANSWERS
1 Yes, they do.
2 They come from before and after Spanish colonial times.
3 They wear them at special festivals.
4 They can carry food, fruit, and babies.
5 Every village has a different hat.
6 Yes, they do.

Extra activity 1
- Give students a few minutes to read the text and to remember as much as they can.
- Books closed. Ask students, in small groups, questions on the text, e.g. *What is a traditional Japanese item of clothing called?* (A kimono) *How much does a kimono cost?* (More than £10,000) *What are the special shoes called in Japan?* (Zori) *How many skirts can a woman wear at a festival in Peru?* (Fifteen) *What are the special shoes called in Peru? (Ojotas).*

Extra activity 2
- Ask the students to think about an occasion when they wore special clothes. It could be for a celebration, a formal or sports event.
- The students make notes about the clothes they wore.
- In pairs, one student describes what he / she wore while the other student draws a picture of the description.
- Students swap roles and repeat the activity.
- Ask a few students to show their drawings to the class and describe what their partner wore.

Project
- Students can do this in class or for homework. It can be done individually, or in pairs / small groups.
- Students design a poster about traditional clothes in their country. Encourage them to find information and to make notes for all the questions on page 68.
- Students produce a rough draft of their poster.
- They can swap drafts with another student / pair / group, who gives feedback and corrects any mistakes.
- Students then produce a final version including photos and illustrations.
- The final posters can be displayed in the classroom.

Workbook answer key

Unit 1

Vocabulary

Adjectives

Exercise 1
(in any order)
terrible   fantastic
boring   interesting
difficult   easy

Exercise 2
Students' own answers

Grammar

be: present simple (Negative)

Exercise 3
1 I'm not Scottish.
2 You aren't funny.
3 John isn't from York.
4 Our homework isn't easy.
5 We aren't German.
6 You aren't students.
7 Anna and Jo aren't sisters.

be: present simple (Interrogative and short answers)

Exercise 4
2 d   3 a   4 e   5 f   6 g   7 b

Exercise 5
1 Are you an Arsenal fan? No, I'm not.
2 Is his car blue? Yes, it is.
3 Are the students at school? Yes, they are.
4 Are they your books? No, they aren't.
5 Are Mike and Paul in the football team? Yes, they are.
6 Is she a new student? Yes, she is.

Question words

Exercise 6
1 Who
2 Where
3 How old
4 What
5 Where
6 When

Exercise 7
1 What   2 Where   3 how   4 What

this, that, these, those

Exercise 8
1 These   2 Those   3 These   4 This

Exercise 9
2 d   3 e   4 a   5 b   6 c

Communication

Asking and answering personal questions

Exercise 1
2 d   3 f   4 a   5 c   6 e

Exercise 2
2 What's your surname?
3 How old are you?
4 What's your address?
5 What's your phone number?
6 What's your email address?

Exercise 3
1 It's Smith.
2 It's Rick.
3 It's 01221 496 0857.
4 It's 16, George Street, Birmingham.

Skills

Reading

Exercise 1
2 Where's he from?
3 When's his birthday?
4 Who are his favourite actors?
5 What are his favourite films?
6 What's his favourite colour?

Exercise 2
1 He isn't from the south-west of England. He's from the south-east of England.
2 His birthday isn't in February. It's in January.
3 His favourite actors aren't Brad Pitt and George Clooney. His favourite actors are Johnny Depp, Paul Newman, and Daniel Day-Lewis.
4 His favourite colour isn't blue. His favourite colour is yellow.

Writing
Students' own answers.

Unit 2

Vocabulary

Family

Exercise 1
1 mum
2 brother
3 aunt
4 cousin

Exercise 2
2 grandma
3 uncle
4 aunt
5 sisters
6 cousin
Mystery word: parents

Grammar

have got: present simple (Affirmative and negative)

Exercise 3
1 've got
2 's got
3 've got
4 's got
5 's got
6 've got

Exercise 4
1 We haven't got an English friend.
2 Ben hasn't got a new teacher.
3 I haven't got a poster of the Jonas Brothers.
4 Fran hasn't got the new Shakira CD.
5 My mobile phone hasn't got a camera.
6 They haven't got a dog.

Exercise 5
1 Jill's got a computer, but she hasn't got a mobile phone.
2 Jess and Liam have got a dog, but they haven't got a cat.
3 Ron and Sue have got skateboards, but they haven't got bikes.
4 Mark's got five cousins, but he hasn't got a brother or a sister.

have got: present simple (Interrogative and short answers)

Exercise 6
1 Have; have
2 Has; hasn't
3 have; haven't
4 Has; has
5 Have; have

Exercise 7
1 Have Liz and Ann got a big family?
  Yes, they have.
2 Has John got a cat?
  No, he hasn't.
3 Has John got a computer?
  Yes, he has.
4 Have Liz and Ann got a cat?
  Yes, they have.
5 Have Liz and Ann got a computer?
  No, they haven't.

Exercise 8
1 Have you got a sister or a brother?
  Yes, I have. / No, I haven't.
2 Have your parents got a car?
  Yes, they have. / No, they haven't.
3 Has your room got a TV?
  Yes, it has. / No, it hasn't.
4 Have you got homework today?
  Yes, I have. / No, I haven't.
5 Have you got cousins?
  Yes, I/we have. / No, I/we haven't.

Possessive *'s*

Exercise 9
1 Martin's
2 the children's
3 the boys'
4 Mario's
5 Paula's
6 Sue and Tim's

Exercise 10
Students' own answers.

Communication

Talking about possessions

Exercise 1
1 Have you got
2 What's your favourite possession
3 Is it new
4 Yes, I have

Exercise 2
1 Yes, it is
2 a camera
3 fantastic
4 No, I haven't
5 It's my MP3 player.
6 it is
7 500 songs on it
8 cool
9 haven't got

Exercise 3
What's your favourite possession?
Is it new?
Students' own answers.

Reading

Exercise 1
1 True.
2 False. Miley Cyrus's real name is Destiny Hope Cyrus.
3 False. Miley's dad is a famous singer and actor.
4 False. Will Smith's wife is an actor.
5 True.
6 False. Jada isn't in *The Pursuit of Happyness.*

Writing

Exercise 2
(possible answer)
… He's an actor and a singer. Miley's mum's name is Leticia. She's Miley's manager. Miley's brother's name's Braison and he's a student. Miley's sister's name is Noah. She's an actor.

Unit 3

Vocabulary

Daily routines

Exercise 1
1 I have a shower at ten to seven.
2 I have breakfast at quarter past seven.
3 I go to school at ten to eight.
4 I have lunch at quarter past one.
5 I get home at four o'clock.
6 I have dinner at half past six.
7 I do my homework at half past seven.
8 I go to bed at ten o'clock.

Exercise 2
1 go
2 have
3 get
4 go
5 get
6 have

Grammar

Present simple (Affirmative)

Exercise 3
1 live
2 They
3 She
4 plays
5 My mum and dad
6 go

Exercise 4
1 play
2 live
3 start
4 visits
5 listen
6 work

Present simple (Spelling variations – 3rd person singular)

Exercise 5
1 watches
2 studies
3 gets up
4 likes
5 has
6 finishes

Exercise 6
1 My sister studies every day.
2 James likes computer games.
3 She watches TV after school.
4 Ali does her homework in the living room.
5 My uncle teaches geography.

Adverbs of frequency

Exercise 7
1 Helen never drinks coffee.
2 We rarely watch TV.
3 She usually goes to bed at eleven o'clock.
4 They're always happy.
5 I'm never late for school.

Prepositions of time

Exercise 8
1 at 2 in 3 at 4 in 5 at 6 in

Exercise 9
1 have; at
2 plays; on
3 is; in
4 go; at
5 do; in

Exercise 10
1 has
2 at
3 in
4 goes
5 works
6 has
7 at
8 in
9 usually finishes
10 at
11 has
12 have
13 go
14 goes
15 get
16 at
17 gets up
18 helps
19 go
20 play

Communication

Talking about TV programmes

Exercise 1
1 day 2 Fridays 3 time
4 8 p.m. 5 channel

Exercise 2
1 7 p.m.
2 Channel 5
3 It's on at 9 p.m.
4 It's on ITV.
5 It's on at 9 p.m.
6 It's on BBC 1.

Exercise 3
Students' own answers.

Skills

Reading

Exercise 1
1 There are eight people in Alanna's family.
2 Alanna's lessons start at 8.30.
3 There are three teachers in Alanna's school. / There are 14 students in Alanna's school.
4 Alanna has lunch at home.
5 Alanna spends her free time with her best friends.

Writing

Exercise 2
Students' own answers.

Unit 4

Vocabulary

Sports

Exercise 1
1 cycling
2 swimming
3 tennis
4 athletics
5 skiing
6 karate
7 basketball
Mystery sport: gymnastics

Exercise 2
(in any order)
go: 1 swimming
        2 skiing
do: 3 athletics
        4 karate
        5 gymnastics
play: 6 tennis
        7 basketball

Grammar

Present simple (Negative)

Exercise 3
1 I
2 doesn't
3 have
4 We
5 don't

Exercise 4
1 We don't go to school on Saturdays.
2 Rachel doesn't do her homework at 4 p.m.
3 Maurizio doesn't go to bed at 11 p.m.
4 Miguel and Pablo don't play basketball.
5 You don't go swimming after school.

Present simple (Interrogative and short answers)

Exercise 5
1 Does; No, she doesn't.
2 Do; Yes, I do.
3 Does; No, he doesn't.
4 Do; Yes, they do.

Exercise 6
1 Does he live in London?
  No, he doesn't.
2 Does he go to school in Bradfield?
  Yes, he does.
3 Does he like sport?
  Yes, he does.
4 Does he play basketball?
  Yes, he does.

Question words + present simple

Exercise 7
1 Where
2 What
3 What
4 When

How often …?

Exercise 8
Students' own answers.

Object pronouns

Exercise 9
1 you
2 him
3 her
4 it
5 us
6 you
7 them

Exercise 10
1 me
2 it
3 her
4 us
5 them
6 him

Communication

Talking about likes and dislikes

Exercise 1
1 I really like Spider-Man. I really like him.
2 I quite like Justin Timberlake. I quite like him.
3 I don't like dogs very much. I don't like them very much.
4 I don't like football at all! I don't like it at all!
5 I hate dentists! I hate them!

Exercise 2
1 Do you like Beyoncé?
2 What do you think of spiders?
3 Do you like Enrique Iglesias?

Exercise 3
Students' own answers.

Skills

Reading

Exercise 1
1 She plays for Scotland.
2 She practises five days a week.
3 She doesn't have any free time on school days.
4 She plays computer games at the weekend.
5 Her dad plays cricket.

Exercise 2
Students' own answers.

Unit 5

Vocabulary

Free-time activities

Exercise 1
a 2 c
  3 a
b 1 c
  2 b
  3 a
c 1 b
  2 c
  3 a
d 1 c
  2 a
  3 b

Exercise 2
1 play
2 read
3 go
4 go
5 ride
6 play
7 go

Grammar

can (ability): Affirmative and negative

Exercise 3
1 ride
2 can
3 swim
4 can
5 can't

Exercise 4
1 can't use
2 can speak
3 can't send
4 can surf

Degrees of ability

Exercise 5
1 Nick can play chess well.
2 Sue can't play chess at all.
3 Nick can swim very well.
4 Sue can swim well.
5 Nick can ski quite well.
6 Sue can ski well.

Exercise 6
Students' own answers.

can (ability): Interrogative and short answers

Exercise 7
1 Can; can
2 Can; can't
3 Can; can
4 Can; can
5 Can; can't
6 Can; can't

Exercise 8
1 I can
2 Can David
3 Yes, she
4 No, they
5 Can you

Imperatives

Exercise 9
2 Don't play; Go
3 Don't talk; Be
4 Don't read; Eat

Exercise 10
1 well
2 sing
3 Phone
4 visit
5 Don't
6 Contact

Communication

Making suggestions

Exercise 1
1 tennis
2 great
3 go
4 bowling
5 bored
6 can

Exercise 2
1 Let's go bowling.
2 play cards
3 go skateboarding

Exercise 3
1
1 What shall we do?
2 Let's go shopping.
3 Good idea!
2
1 I'm really bored. Let's play cards.
2 No, I don't like cards.
3 Let's go skateboarding, then.
4 OK, great.

Skills

Reading

Exercise 1
1 True.
2 True.
3 False. He can play the cello and the piano.
4 False. He writes music for all instruments.
5 True.

Writing

Exercise 2
1 sing
2 musical instruments
3 well
4 basketball
5 do gymnastics
6 gold medal

Unit 6

Vocabulary

Clothes

Exercise 1
1 skirt
2 jacket
3 dress
4 jumper
5 shirt
6 trousers

Exercise 2
Students' own answers.

Grammar

Present continuous (Affirmative)

Exercise 3
1 is
2 are
3 am
4 is
5 are
6 am

Present continuous (Spelling variations)

Exercise 4
1 listening
2 playing
3 running
4 singing
5 sitting
6 stopping
7 studying
8 using

Exercise 5
1 reading
2 using
3 surfing
4 eating
5 writing
6 running

Negative

Exercise 6
1 Sarah and Jo aren't doing their homework. They're watching TV.
2 Christopher isn't having breakfast. He's having dinner.
3 Janet isn't writing an email. She's writing a letter.
4 Gary isn't reading a comic. He's listening to music.
5 Mr Jackson isn't driving his car. He's riding a bike.
6 Emily and Paul aren't going to the sports centre. They're going to the cinema.

Present continuous (Interrogative and short answers)

Exercise 7
1 Are they going to school? Yes, they are.
2 Is she wearing a skirt? No, she isn't.
3 Are the students doing a test? No, they aren't.
4 Is Mr Taylor writing his emails? Yes, he is.

Exercise 8
1 'm washing
2 's using
3 's writing
4 Is … watching
5 's sleeping

Question words + present continuous

Exercise 9
1 What's he writing?
  He's writing
2 Who's she talking to?
  She's talking to
3 Where's he sleeping?
  He's sleeping
4 What are they watching?
  They're watching

Communication

Money and shopping for clothes

Exercise 1
1 twenty-two pounds twenty (pence / p)
2 fifteen pounds ninety-nine (pence / p)
3 one hundred and three pounds forty (pence / p)
4 fifty-five pence / p
5 forty-five pounds twenty (pence / p)

Exercise 2
1 It's £22.50.
2 I'm a small.
3 They're too big.

Exercise 3
1 Can I help you?
2 Yes, please. How much is this jumper?
3 It's £35.
4 Can I try it on?
5 Yes, of course. What size are you?
6 I'm a medium.
7 Here you are. How does it fit?
8 It's perfect. I'll take it.

Exercise 4
Students' own answers.

Skills

Reading

Exercise 1
1 He usually wears a shirt, trousers, and shoes to school.
2 He's riding his bike.
3 He's wearing a blue T-shirt, his favourite orange and blue cap, jeans, and trainers.
4 She's wearing her school uniform.
5 They wear a blue jacket, grey trousers, and a white shirt.

Writing

Exercise 2
Students' own answers.

Wordlist

This wordlist shows the new key words and phrases that are introduced in *Champions* Starter level. The words are presented alphabetically and followed by a reference to where each is introduced.

Key: W = Welcome, U = Unit, R = Review, Cc = Culture club, Ce = Curriculum extra

Word	Translation / Definition

Aa

act U3 _____

actor U1 _____

Argentina W _____

Argentinian W _____

Chile W _____

Chilean W _____

address U1 _____

after U3 _____

afternoon U3 _____

also U3 _____

always U3 _____

amazing U2 _____

American W _____

apple W _____

April W _____

arrive U5 _____

art CeB _____

athletics U4 _____

audition U1 _____

August W _____

aunt U2 _____

Australia W _____

Australian W _____

autumn W _____

Bb

baby W _____

back CeC _____

badminton U6 _____

ball U5 _____

ballet U4 _____

band U1 _____

basketball U4 _____

be W _____

beach U6 _____

beautiful CeA _____

become U5 _____

bedroom U3 _____

before U3 _____

bend CeB _____

big CeA _____

bike U2 _____

biology CeB _____

birthday W _____

biscuit CeC _____

Word	Translation / Definition

black W _____

blue W _____

body CeB _____

bone CeB _____

book W _____

boring U1 _____

boss U2 _____

box W _____

boy U3 _____

Brazil W _____

Brazilian W _____

brilliant U5 _____

British W _____

brother W _____

brown W _____

building U5 _____

bus W _____

busy U5 _____

Cc

cake U5 _____

camera phone U2 _____

camp U6 _____

Canada W _____

Canadian W _____

cap U6 _____

capital city W _____

cardiac muscle CeB _____

cartoon U2 _____

cat U2 _____

CD U2 _____

celebrate U6 _____

celebrity U2 _____

century CeC _____

chair U5 _____

champion U1 _____

changing room U6 _____

channel U3 _____

character U3 _____

chef U1 _____

child W _____

China W _____

Chinese W _____

chocolate U6 _____

choice U2 _____

cinema U1 _____

Word	Translation / Definition
city U5	
class W	
classical music U1	
climb U5	
cloth CeC	
club CeC	
cold CeB	
collar CeC	
Colombia W	
Colombian W	
colonial CeC	
combination CeC	
come U5	
computer U1	
concert U2	
cook CeC	
cool U1	
corridor U5	
cost CeC	
cousin U2	
craft U6	
crayon W	
crazy U1	
cricket U6	
cry U3	
custom CeA	
cycle U6	
cycling U4	

Dd

dad U2	
dance U1	
dancer U3	
danger U5	
dark U5	
daughter U2	
December W	
dedicate U4	
delicious U1	
design and technology CeB	
design CeC	
desk W	
different U3	
difficult U1	
digital camera U2	
disco U6	
discover U5	
do my homework U3	
do U3	
dog U2	
drama U1	
dream U4	

Word	Translation / Definition
dress U6	
DVD player U2	

Ee

east U3	
easy U1	
eccentric U2	
eight W	
eighteen W	
electronic CeC	
eleven W	
email address U1	
ethnic CeA	
evening U3	
exam U4	
exercise book W	
exercise CeB	
expensive CeC	

Ff

family W	
famous U2	
fan W	
fantastic W	
fashion show U6	
fast U5	
favourite U1	
February W	
felt tip W	
festival CeC	
fifteen W	
film U2	
finish U3	
five past W	
five to W	
five W	
fly U5	
food U1	
football W	
forest CeA	
four W	
fourteen W	
free U3	
French W	
Friday W	
friend W	
front CeC	
fruit CeC	
frustrated U4	
fun U3	
funny U1	

Word   Translation / Definition

Gg

games console U2 _____
garden U1 _____
geography U1 _____
German U4 _____
get home U3 _____
get up U3 _____
girl W _____
go back U4 _____
go bowling U5 _____
go out CeC _____
go shopping U5 _____
go skateboarding U5 _____
go to bed U3 _____
go to school U3 _____
go to the cinema U5 _____
go U3 _____
goal U4 _____
gold U4 _____
golf U6 _____
grandad U2 _____
grandma U2 _____
grandparents U2 _____
grandson U2 _____
great U2 _____
Greece W _____
Greek W _____
green W _____
group CeA _____
gym U3 _____
gymnastics U4 _____

Hh

hair U2 _____
half past W _____
happen U6 _____
happy U3 _____
hat CeC _____
hate U4 _____
have a shower U3 _____
have breakfast U3 _____
have dinner U3 _____
have lunch U3 _____
head teacher U1 _____
hip hop U3 _____
history CeB _____
hobby U5 _____
holiday U6 _____
host family U3 _____
house U3 _____
hurry up U5 _____
husband U2 _____

Word   Translation / Definition

Ii

ice cream W _____
ideal U2 _____
important CeA _____
in secret U3 _____
information and communication technologies (I.C.T.) CeB _____
instrument U5 _____
intelligent U5 _____
interesting U1 _____
Internet U2 _____
item CeC _____

Jj

jacket U6 _____
January W _____
Japan W _____
Japanese W _____
jazz U1 _____
job U2 _____
joke U4 _____
July W _____
jump U5 _____
jumper U6 _____
June W _____

Kk

karaoke U6 _____
karate U4 _____
kayaking U6 _____
kimono CeC _____
kitchen U3 _____

Ll

language CeA _____
laptop U2 _____
large U6 _____
laser U2 _____
late U5 _____
learn U6 _____
leave U6 _____
lesson U1 _____
letter U3 _____
library U6 _____
like U4 _____
listen U3 _____
live U3 _____
living room U3 _____
local U1 _____
look U1 _____
love U4 _____

Word	Translation / Definition

Mm

make U6 _____
man W _____
March W _____
material CeC _____
maths W _____
May W _____
medal U4 _____
medium U6 _____
member U2 _____
metre U4 _____
Mexican W _____
Mexico W _____
million CcA _____
miss U3 _____
mobile U1 _____
Monday W _____
morning U3 _____
MP3 player U2 _____
mum U2 _____
muscle CeB _____
music U1 _____
musical U1 _____

Nn

name W _____
never U3 _____
new U2 _____
newspaper U6 _____
night U3 _____
nine W _____
nineteen W _____
normal U4 _____
north U1 _____
November W _____

Oo

o'clock W _____
October W _____
official CeA _____
often U3 _____
one W _____
only child U2 _____
opera U1 _____
orange W _____
organ CeB _____
orienteering U6 _____
original U2 _____

Pp

parents U2 _____
park U3 _____
part U3 _____

Word	Translation / Definition

passion U1 _____
past CeC _____
pasta U1 _____
peasant CeC _____
pen W _____
pencil case W _____
pencil sharpener W _____
pencil W _____
penfriend U2 _____
perfect U2 _____
person W _____
phone U1 _____
photo CeB _____
physical education (P.E.) CeB _____
piano U4 _____
piece CeC _____
pink W _____
pizza U4 _____
planet U5 _____
play cards U5 _____
play chess U5 _____
play computer games U5 _____
play the guitar U5 _____
play U3 _____
player U1 _____
poncho CeC _____
popular U2 _____
population CeA _____
possession U2 _____
postcard U6 _____
poster U1 _____
power U5 _____
prefer U4 _____
present CeC _____
production U3 _____
programme U3 _____
protect U5 _____
proud U3 _____
purple W _____

Qq

quarter past W _____
quarter to W _____
Quechuan CeC _____
quite U4 _____
quiz U6 _____

Rr

rain U6 _____
rarely U3 _____
read comics U5 _____
read U3 _____
real life U2 _____

Word	Translation / Definition	Word	Translation / Definition

Word   Translation / Definition

reality programme U4 _____

really U4 _____

red W _____

represent U4 _____

ride a bike U5 _____

ring U4 _____

rock U6 _____

rubber W _____

rucksack W _____

ruler W _____

run U5 _____

Russia W _____

Russian W _____

Ss

sandcastle U6 _____

sandwich W _____

Saturday W _____

saxophone U1 _____

say U3 _____

school uniform CeB _____

school W _____

schoolboy U3 _____

science U4 _____

seaside U6 _____

secretary U1 _____

see U5 _____

send text messages U5 _____/

sensation U3 _____

September W _____

series U5 _____

serious U1 _____

seven W _____

seventeen W _____

shape CeB _____

shirt U6 _____

shoes U6 _____

shorts U6 _____

shoulder CeC _____

shout U6 _____

show U3 _____

sing U3 _____

singer W _____

sister U2 _____

sit U6 _____

six W _____

sixteen W _____

size U6 _____

skateboard U2 _____

skeletal muscle CeB _____

ski U5 _____

skiing U4 _____

skirt U6 _____

Word   Translation / Definition

sleep U3 _____

sleeve CeC _____

small U2 _____

smooth muscle CeB _____

soap opera U4 _____

social science CeA _____

sometimes U3 _____

son U2 _____

song U2 _____

South Africa W _____

South African W _____

South Korea W _____

South Korean W _____

south U1 _____

Spain W _____

Spanish W _____

speak U3 _____

special U4 _____

spell W _____

spider U4 _____

sports centre U4 _____

spring W _____

staff U1 _____

stand up U6 _____

star U1 _____

start U5 _____

stay CeC _____

stomach CeB _____

stop U6 _____

story U3 _____

stretch CeB _____

strict U1 _____

strong U5 _____

student W _____

study U3 _____

style CeC _____

subject U4 _____

success U4 _____

summer W _____

sunbathe U6 _____

Sunday W _____

superhero U5 _____

superpower U5 _____

surf the Internet U5 _____

surname W _____

swimming pool U4 _____

swimming U4 _____

Tt

take U6 _____

talent contest U6 _____

talk CeC _____

teach U4 _____

Word	Translation / Definition
teacher W	_____
teenager U4	_____
ten past W	_____
ten to W	_____
ten W	_____
tennis U4	_____
terrible U1	_____
the United Kingdom (UK) W	_____
the United States (US) W	_____
theatre U1	_____
thirteen W	_____
thirty W	_____
three W	_____
Thursday W	_____
ticket U2	_____
tidy U3	_____
tissue CeB	_____
today U5	_____
together U2	_____
tomato W	_____
tomorrow U5	_____
top U6	_____
tournament U6	_____
town CeA	_____
tradition CeA	_____
trainers U6	_____
trampolining U6	_____
treasure hunt U6	_____
tribe CeA	_____
trousers U6	_____
true U2	_____
try on U6	_____
T-shirt U6	_____
Tuesday W	_____
twelve W	_____
twenty past W	_____
twenty to W	_____
twenty W	_____
twenty-five past W	_____
twenty-five to W	_____
two W	_____
type CeB	_____
typical U3	_____

Uu

umbrella W	_____
uncle U2	_____
university W	_____
use U6	_____
usually U6	_____

Word	Translation / Definition

Vv

very U4	_____
Vietnam W	_____
Vietnamese W	_____
village CeC	_____
violin U5	_____
visit U3	_____

Ww

wall U5	_____
warm up CeB	_____
watch out U1	_____
watch U3	_____
wear U6	_____
web U5	_____
Wednesday W	_____
weekend U3	_____
white W	_____
win U4	_____
winter W	_____
woman W	_____
woollen CeC	_____
work U4	_____
world U6	_____
write U3	_____

Xx

X-ray vision U5	_____

Yy

year U1	_____
yellow W	_____

Portfolio

Speaking and writing

1 I can talk about my favourite things.   A1

My favourite band is The Script.

1 _____
2 _____
3 _____
4 _____
5 _____

Can you? ___ / 5

2 I can give my opinion about people and things.   A1

Jack Black is funny.

1 _____
2 _____
3 _____
4 _____
5 _____

Can you? ___ / 5

3 I can ask and answer questions about another person.   A1

Where is Holly from? She's from Scotland.

1 _____
2 _____
3 _____
4 _____
5 _____

Can you? ___ / 5

4 I can identify people in a family.   A1

mother

1 _____
2 _____
3 _____
4 _____
5 _____

Can you? ___ / 5

5 Answer questions about people in my family.   A1

Charlie is my uncle.

1 _____
2 _____
3 _____
4 _____
5 _____

Can you? ___ / 5

6 I can identify objects and people by asking questions.   A1

What's this? / Who's Jacob?

1 _____
2 _____
3 _____
4 _____
5 _____

Can you? ___ / 5

Reading, listening, and writing

		Can you?	
	Yes	I'm not sure	No
7 I can understand basic information about people. A1	☐	☐	☐
8 I can write a description of a person. A1	☐	☐	☐
9 I can complete a family tree. A1	☐	☐	☐
10 I can read about different people in families. A1	☐	☐	☐

Portfolio

Speaking and writing

1 I can talk about my daily routine to my partner. **A1**

I get up at seven o'clock.

1 _____
2 _____
3 _____
4 _____
5 _____

Can you? ____ / 5

2 I can say when I do things. **A1**

I watch TV in the evening.

1 _____
2 _____
3 _____
4 _____
5 _____

Can you? ____ / 5

3 I can talk about my favourite TV shows. **A1**

My favourite TV programme is House.

1 _____
2 _____
3 _____
4 _____
5 _____

Can you? ____ / 5

4 I can talk about how often and when I play sports. **A1**

I sometimes play tennis.

1 _____
2 _____
3 _____
4 _____
5 _____

Can you? ____ / 5

5 I can ask questions about sports. **A1**

Do you play basketball?

1 _____
2 _____
3 _____
4 _____
5 _____

Can you? ____ / 5

6 I can talk about likes and dislikes. **A1**

I quite like 50 Cent.

1 _____
2 _____
3 _____
4 _____
5 _____

Can you? ____ / 5

Reading, listening, and writing

		Can you?		
		Yes	I'm not sure	No
7 I can write about my daily routine.	A1	☐	☐	☐
8 I can understand and complete information about a dancer.	A1	☐	☐	☐
9 I can write about different sports.	A1	☐	☐	☐
10 I can understand and answer questions about a swimmer.	A1	☐	☐	☐

Portfolio

Speaking and writing

1 I can identify free-time activities. **A1**

go shopping

1 _____
2 _____
3 _____
4 _____
5 _____

Can you? ____ / 5

2 I can describe things I can and can't do. **A2**

I can speak English well.

1 _____
2 _____
3 _____
4 _____
5 _____

Can you? ____ / 5

3 I can ask and answer questions about what my family and friends can do. **A2**

My sister can't play the piano very well.

1 _____
2 _____
3 _____
4 _____
5 _____

Can you? ____ / 5

4 I can make suggestions. **A2**

Why don't we go shopping?

1 _____
2 _____
3 _____
4 _____
5 _____

Can you? ____ / 5

5 I can ask and answer questions about what people are doing. **A2**

What's Tom doing?

1 _____
2 _____
3 _____
4 _____
5 _____

Can you? ____ / 5

6 I can ask how much clothes cost. **A2**

How much are these trousers?

1 _____
2 _____
3 _____
4 _____
5 _____

Can you? ____ / 5

Reading, listening, and writing

		Can you?		
		Yes	I'm not sure	No
7 I can understand a text about superheroes and what they can and can't do.	**A2**	☐	☐	☐
8 I can describe clothes and talk about what people are wearing.	**A2**	☐	☐	☐
9 I can understand an e mail.	**A2**	☐	☐	☐
10 I can write a postcard.	**A2**	☐	☐	☐

UNIVERSITY PRESS

Great Clarendon Street, Oxford OX2 6DP

Oxford University Press is a department of the University of Oxford.
It furthers the University's objective of excellence in research, scholarship,
and education by publishing worldwide in

Oxford New York

Auckland Cape Town Dar es Salaam Hong Kong Karachi
Kuala Lumpur Madrid Melbourne Mexico City Nairobi
New Delhi Shanghai Taipei Toronto

With offices in

Argentina Austria Brazil Chile Czech Republic France Greece
Guatemala Hungary Italy Japan Poland Portugal Singapore
South Korea Switzerland Thailand Turkey Ukraine Vietnam

OXFORD and OXFORD ENGLISH are registered trade marks of
Oxford University Press in the UK and in certain other countries

ISBN: 978 0 19 400429 9

Printed in China

This book is printed on paper from certified and well-managed sources.